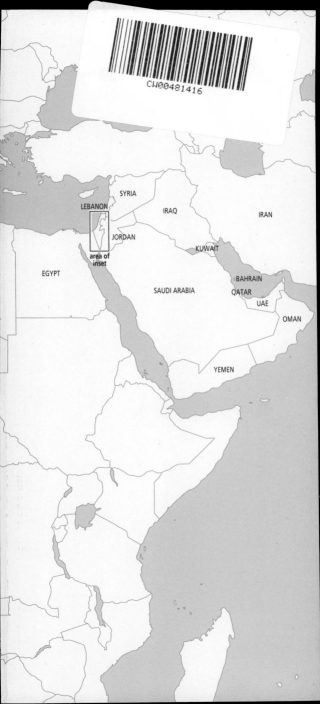

SYRIA

LEBANON

IRAQ

IRAN

JORDAN

area of
inset

KUWAIT

EGYPT

BAHRAIN

QATAR

SAUDI ARABIA

UAE

OMAN

YEMEN

The Economist

POCKET MIDDLE EAST AND NORTH AFRICA

The
Economist

POCKET

MIDDLE

EAST

AND

NORTH

AFRICA

Roland Dallas

THE ECONOMIST IN ASSOCIATION WITH
HAMISH HAMILTON LTD

Published by the Penguin Group
Penguin Books Ltd, 27 Wrights Lane, London W8 5TZ, England
Penguin Books USA Inc., 375 Hudson Street, New York,
New York 10014, USA
Penguin Books Australia Ltd, Ringwood, Victoria, Australia
Penguin Books Canada Ltd, 10 Alcorn Avenue, Toronto,
Ontario, Canada M4V 3B2
Penguin Books (NZ) Ltd, 182–190 Wairau Road, Auckland 10,
New Zealand

Penguin Books Ltd, Registered Offices: Harmondsworth,
Middlesex, England

First published by Hamish Hamilton Ltd in association
with The Economist Books 1995

10 9 8 7 6 5 4 3 2 1

Copyright © The Economist Books Ltd, 1995

Text copyright © Roland Dallas, 1995
Additional research: Peter Holden

Printed in Great Britain by
William Clowes Limited, Beccles, Suffolk

A CIP catalogue record for this book is available
from the British Library

ISBN 0-241-13513-3

Contents

INTRODUCTION

In the mid-1990s vital questions about the future of the Middle East went unanswered. To what extent would Islam play a part in Arab governments? How democratic would they be? What sort of relationship would they have with Israel? What would happen, if peace broke out, to regional co-operation, arms reduction and free trade? Iran had to decide between continued support for violent extremists and international support for its ailing economy. Iraq had to decide whether or not to accept all the terms of the ultimatum of the UN Security Council after Iraqi forces were ousted from Kuwait. Which way would they go?

How fundamental?

In 1979 Ayatollah Khomeini and his men rose up against established authority in Iran, overthrew the shah and imposed Islam as a central force guiding not only religious teaching but also public and private morality, government, foreign affairs and the clothes people wore. It may be that this wave of Islamic puritanism will eventually be succeeded by a more open and tolerant attitude. But in the mid-1990s the fundamentalist wave was still surging. The great issue before the Middle Eastern countries was: would this wave sweep across the region? It was no accident that at the same time the Christian West was marked by sceptical liberalism and permissive standards of behaviour which Islamists found shocking and corrupt. They decided to fight its spread to the Muslim world.

Different approaches

Islam has many faces. At the end of one spectrum is Iran's Islamic Republic, whose supreme chief is the *wali faqhi* (religious leader), Ayatollah Khamenei, who is himself guided by a committee of senior clerics. Below him comes Iran's president, Ali Akbar Hashemi Rafsanjani, who holds the lower clerical rank of *hojatoleslam*. At the other end of this spectrum is Turkey, a Muslim country with a secular state. The government controls the clerics and not, as in Iran, the other way round. In Algeria secular leaders and Islamists have been locked in a bloody struggle for power. Islam has other faces: the two great religious traditions followed by the Sunnis and the Shia and also smaller groups such as the sternly puritanical Wahabis of Saudi Arabia and the Alawite sect of Syria. These traditions have become deeply entrenched over the centuries; there is little prospect of a wave of ecumenism.

Two extremes

All the signs were that the leaders of the Middle East had learnt the lesson of history. They had observed the rise and fall of the shah of Iran. They had seen him prosper, as the world oil price increased, and try too speedily to modernise and westernise a poor and under-developed country with deeply ingrained religious traditions. The shah did not take Islam sufficiently into account. His neglect was lethal ammunition for Ayatollah Khomeini and his followers. The Middle East's new leaders realised that the shah's approach had to be avoided at all costs. They also rejected the other extreme: Iran's way of propagating its theocratic ideas and its support of violent extremists in the region. They sought the answer somewhere in the middle, in a display of devout belief, a dash of democracy and secular government.

The middle way

King Hassan of Morocco, for example, says he is a descendant of the Prophet Muhammad, calls himself the "Commander of the Faithful" and has built the world's biggest mosque in Casablanca. The astute Hassan has made it difficult for the Islamists to challenge his religious credentials. However, the king is a worldly man with a penchant for palaces and golf, and his parliament is composed of secular political parties and independents who enjoy a lively debate. The leading Islamist is under house arrest. Barring the unexpected, the middle way seems to be working for the king.

In Egypt extreme Islamists are hunted down. Some established opposition parties in Egypt are, however, increasingly reflecting Islamist ideas while falling short of calling for the establishment of an Islamic republic; they are not repressed but have no chance of gaining a share of power. But President Hosni Mubarak insists that radio stations frequently broadcast sermons to prove his Islamic credentials.

King Hussein of Jordan, a past master at bending with the prevailing wind, invited Islamists elected to parliament to join a coalition. They did so, and since the government was applying an austerity programme, lost credibility. King Hussein makes frequent references to God's will in his speeches.

King Fahd of Saudi Arabia invariably bears the title "Guardian of the Two Holy Mosques" (in Mecca and Medina). His family behaves in public according to the strict rules of Wahabi Islam. Saudi oil riches have been spread around, not only to hundreds of members of one family but also to the people through the services of a generous welfare state, partly in order to destroy the case for change or reform. But, to Iran's disgust, Saudi Arabia is a family-run kingdom, not an Islamic republic. Fundamentalists have been circulating cassettes containing anti-government sermons and some have been arrested. Barring an upset, the royal family seems to be secure for the foreseeable future.

How democratic?

The Arab world is not particularly democratic. Nonetheless, a slow democratic opening is taking place as society evolves. It is slow because it is a new experience for many. Poor standards of education are being improved in oil-financed welfare states. Education will make increasing numbers of people aware of political freedoms in other parts of the world. The message comes through, loud, clear and in colour, on satellite television news services. Many sons and daughters of the upper and middle classes in the Middle East go to university in Britain, the United States, France and elsewhere in the West. Many go home having imbibed deep draughts of democracy.

Strongmen are now on the defensive. After the American-led "coalition" forces liberated Kuwait from the grip of Iraq's Saddam Hussein, the emir came under strong international pressure to hold new parliamentary elections, which he did. Many Middle Eastern rulers found they had to defend themselves against criticism from groups such as Amnesty International and the New York-based Human Rights Watch. With Latin America and Eastern Europe having become mostly democratic, the spotlight was turning uncomfortably on to the Middle East (and to a lesser extent on Africa and Asia).

Up to a point

The degree of Middle Eastern democracy varies widely. But so far no country has passed the litmus test: the holding of a free and fair election which the opposition wins, and a peaceful transfer of power that takes place on the appointed date. Presidential elections are held, but the incumbent usually wins with more than 90% of the vote (for example, Presidents Mubarak of Egypt, Ben Ali of Tunisia and Assad of Syria). Parliamentary elections are held, many of them free and fair, but opposition candidates are sometimes split into disorganised factions or obliged to stand as individuals rather than as representatives of parties. In many Middle Eastern countries no elections are held at all. The strongmen may argue that they should stay strong for fear of the spread of Islamic fundamentalism. But the evidence, especially in Morocco and Jordan, suggests that good governance and a relatively democratic set-up, in which the people have a clear opportunity to let off steam when they are dissatisfied, is the best antidote to extremism. The trouble is that western governments are not prepared to put pressure on Middle Eastern leaders to open up their political life because they fear it will be swiftly occupied by the Islamists, as happened in Algeria. The West's great fear is that this might happen in Egypt.

Algeria is no model

Middle Eastern leaders have little to learn from Algeria because, with the exception of Egypt, its history is unlike theirs. First, after independence it stagnated under the dead hand of state socialism. There was no private investment worth talking about. Private initiative went unrewarded. Second, it has lived since independence under the authoritarian rule of a military-led regime which muffled dissent. Third, although it has oil and gas it is no Saudi Arabia and cannot spend billions of dollars on a welfare state. Fourth, it has big cities such as Algiers, Oran, Constantine and Annaba, whose populations cannot be sustained by the decaying economy. The two key comparisons with Egypt are not close: although Egypt's economy also stagnated for years, it is now increasingly in the hands of energetic entrepreneurs; and its political life and level of public debate is lively and sophisticated. There was no comparison between the occasional attacks by extremists on tourists in Egypt and the systematic attempt to kill all foreigners in Algeria.

Safety first

Nonetheless, the twin experiences of Iran and Algeria gave most Middle Eastern rulers a reason for not delegating power in a hurry. This was not the case with Morocco (next door to Algeria), where King Hassan asked the opposition in 1994 to propose to him their choice of a parliamentarian who would become prime minister. Nor was it the case in Jordan, where the king, in signing a peace treaty with Israel, had wide parliamentary support. In the Gulf in the mid-1990s, Kuwait was planning its second general election since liberation from Iraqi occupation. Oman had an appointed Consultative Council which could question ministers; its proceedings were televised. The United Arab Emirates had its appointed Federal National Council, which could be consulted on legislation before it was examined by the appointed Council of Ministers. Even the Saudis had their appointed Consultative Council.

Such councils can evolve in two ways. They can be either figleafs hiding the naked use of power by ruling families or the first tentative stage on the road to genuine parliaments with power to legislate (while remaining loyal to constitutional monarchs). Curiously, Iran's parliament is a lively affair. Although large sections of Iranian society, especially those opposed to an Islamic republic, are excluded, parliament frequently challenges the president and has rejected his budget and a choice for finance minister.

As things stand, however, government in much of the Middle East is a family affair. All through the Gulf cabinets are packed with rulers' sons, brothers, uncles and other family members. (These cabinets never include the rulers' daughters, sisters or aunts, a clear demonstration that the Middle East has not yet graduated to the class of Turkey and Pakistan, two Muslim countries whose prime ministers in 1995 were women.) In Iraq almost all key posts were held by close relations of President Saddam Hussein or at least members of his al-Tikriti clan. Syria's President Assad had been grooming his eldest son to succeed him. When he was killed in a car crash, the president turned his attention to a younger son.

Dealing with Israel

In the Middle East peace process, the tide appeared to turn in 1994. First the Palestine Liberation Organisation (PLO) made peace with Israel and took over the Israeli-controlled Gaza strip and the small town of Jericho on the West Bank. The PLO's chairman, Yasser Arafat, became president of the Palestinian Authority, which was due to take over the rest of the West Bank (some Israeli settlements excluded) and hold elections to a Palestinian assembly. Next came peace between Israel and Jordan, with the promise of close economic co-operation. After that on the agenda was peace between Israel and both Syria and Lebanon. Under a deal with Syria, Israel would hand back the formerly Syrian Golan Heights in return for peace and full diplomatic and trade relations. With Lebanon, Israel was seeking full diplomatic and trade relations as well as a guarantee that the anti-Israeli guerrillas in the south would stop shelling its northern communities. In return Israel would withdraw from the "security zone" it had established in Lebanon north of the Israeli border, and close down the "South Lebanon Army", its mainly Christian militia there. The widely held assumption in 1994 was that Israel would make peace with

Syria and Lebanon in 1995, prior to the election campaigns in Israel and the United States in 1996.

With these two pacts, an overall Middle East peace settlement would be in place. That, at least, was the hope. By early 1995, however, negotiators were finding that "the devil is in the details". Reflecting Israeli voters' fears for their security against terrorism, the government was holding back from handing over more of the West Bank to the Palestine Authority and from withdrawing its troops prior to an election. Reflecting popular distrust of Syria, Israel was holding back from promising a full withdrawal from the Golan Heights, Syria's condition for holding formal peace talks. By early 1995 peace still seemed within reach, but also seemed to be receding. Action was urgently needed.

In the same bed

The peoples of the Levant are traders and manufacturers *par excellence*. They have never had the opportunity to deploy all their talents to the full. After long years of rule by the slothful Ottomans came the British mandate and the Jewish immigrants, the establishment of the State of Israel, and conflict. What kind of peace would it be? Certainly not the "cold peace" that has existed between Egypt and Israel since the two countries settled their differences at Camp David in 1979 watched by the benevolent and determined Jimmy Carter. Egypt had held back from cosying up to Israel while there was no peace between the Jewish state and its neighbours and the PLO. President Mubarak has never forgotten the fate of Anwar Sadat, his brave predecessor, who in 1977 flew to Jerusalem and addressed the Israeli parliament and two years later signed the Camp David agreement bringing peace to Egypt and Israel and establishing a framework for negotiations for a wider peace. Sadat was assassinated in 1981.

Assuming a trouble-free transition, peace would mean a surge in trade. Airline services between Israel and its neighbours would start or expand. The railway line between Tel Aviv and Beirut, blocked at an Israel-Lebanon border tunnel, could reopen; so could all the bridges across the Jordan river. Agreement had already been reached on access to the waters of the Jordan by Israel and Jordan. Some big projects in and around Israel were being discussed: an Aqaba-Eilat-Cairo highway; an Amman-Jericho-Jerusalem highway; an Egypt-Gaza gas pipeline; an electricity-grid link-up; a Dead Sea-Red Sea canal; and a Dead Sea-Mediterranean canal.

In the wider Middle East, ideas were circulating for closer co-operation on vital water resources; on maritime pollution, sewage and desertification; on refugees; and on arms reduction. There would be disputes, but they would be mostly trade disputes, over tariffs and other such issues, and arguments over the allocation of resources. These would be handled normally – after all, had not Arabs and Jews lived alongside each other in the Arab world ever since the dispersal of the Jews at the end of the second commonwealth in about 70 AD?

The enemies of peace

Although most people stood to benefit from a peace settlement, it still had enemies. Among them were Palestinian extremists who thought Yasser Arafat's step-by-step agreement was a sell-out. They stood ready to cause an incident that would wreck the peace process. A bloody terrorist attack by a suicide bomber, or an assassination, might possibly turn the Israeli public against a deal with Syria. The peace process might suffer a near-mortal blow. Who would do it?

First, the secretive military wing of the Palestinian Islamist organisation Hamas. It is known as the Brigades of Ezzeldin Qassem, after an Arab nationalist leader killed by the British in 1935. The Brigades had a skilled bomb-maker, nicknamed "the engineer", and volunteers ready to commit suicide by detonating the bomb they were carrying while on a crowded Israeli bus. Brigades fighters are well trained and daring. On at least one occasion they mounted an attack wearing Israeli army uniforms. On another they dressed as religious Jews. On at least two occasions they killed members of Israel's security service, Shin Bet: one was talking to a Palestinian informer; the other was on his way to a rendez-vous with one.

The opponents of peace also include Syria-based enemies of Mr Arafat such as Ahmed Jibril, George Habash and Abu Musa as well as the elusive arch-terrorist Abu Nidal. But the anti-Israeli militia in south Lebanon, Hizbullah, appeared ready to accept a peace settlement provided that it included an Israeli withdrawal from its "security zone" in south Lebanon. If that happened, Hizbullah would hang up its Kalashnikovs and concentrate on its non-violent life in Lebanese civilian politics – or so it said.

The Palestine question

Although a framework for peace between Israel and the Palestinians existed – the Declaration of Principles signed in Norway – much remained to be hammered out. The Palestinians were certain to press for some sort of authority over

Arab East Jerusalem, which the Israelis captured in 1967, and the Israelis equally certainly were bound to argue that Jerusalem was indivisible. The powers of the Palestinian Authority would certainly be an issue: the Palestinians wanted their new parliament to have legislative as well as administrative powers; the Israelis were ready to cede power by degrees. The Israelis were bound to want to protect the rights of thousands of settlers in the West Bank under Israeli laws; the Palestinians would want their own courts to have authority. Most important, it was not clear exactly what status the West Bank and Gaza strip would have. The Palestinians wanted their own state. The Israelis were uneasy. Mr Arafat's negotiators were firm. But Hamas, which had articulate civilian leaders as well as murderous military ones, was more hardline. The Hamas men wanted to move faster to full independence. Hamas was certain to present a challenge to the PLO in any election and to make a good showing.

The Iraqi dilemma

In late 1994 Iraq seemed to be on its last legs, hammered by UN trade sanctions following its disastrous and unsuccessful invasion of Kuwait. Many Iraqis were unemployed, hungry and lacking medicines. Yet President Saddam Hussein chose this moment to mass troops near the Kuwaiti border. President Clinton promptly sent hundreds of American troops to Kuwait and Britain sent a small but symbolic contingent. Saddam Hussein withdrew. The only sensible explanation for the Iraqi dictator's behaviour was that he was huffing and puffing before making concessions to the UN Security Council.

After Iraq's forces were ousted from Kuwait in 1991, the Security Council made four demands. Iraq must give up "weapons of mass destruction" and the means to make them, to the satisfaction of UN inspectors; recognise Kuwait and its newly demarcated frontier; hand over several hundred Kuwaiti prisoners of war; and pay reparations first to the UN to cover its costs, and second to Kuwait to cover the cost of the damage the occupation caused. In return Iraq could resume pumping oil. The Security Council also ruled that Iraq could in any event export limited amounts of oil under UN supervision to pay for food and medicine as well as reparations. Saddam Hussein rejected this offer, and the Iraqis suffered for it. But he recognised Kuwait and its border. He seemed ready to hand over some prisoners. And the UN inspectors were in the final stages of their work, putting a permanent inspection system in place.

By early 1995 there had been no breakthrough. If Iraq was allowed to resume exporting oil, however, it would depress the world price and reduce the earnings of other oil-producing countries. The economies of most of the Gulf oil producers were sound but Saudi Arabia was already suffering a large budget deficit and was late with many of its payments for imports. It was in the interest of oil producers around the world that sanctions on Iraqi oil exports remained in place as long as possible. It was also in the interest of some western countries, such as the United States, that the sanctions remain in place until they led to the downfall of Saddam Hussein. It was not, however, in the interest of Russia and France: they were owed huge sums of money for purchases of arms and other goods and for half-finished projects: these bills would be paid only after Iraq resumed exporting oil.

The Iranian unknown

As Iran's Islamic government evolved, it had to choose between two paths: to support violent Islamic extremists and oppose the Middle East peace process; or to gain international respectability and loans for its faltering economy. Not surprisingly Iran's rulers seemed to want to have their cake and eat it. Several European countries rescheduled Iran's debts without, apparently, exacting a *quid pro quo* of non-extremist future behaviour. That situation was unlikely to continue as more debts fell due. Iran had already changed.

In 1994 there were no acts of terrorism directly linked to the Tehran government. That was progress. But Iran's leaders denounced the peace process and gave at least moral encouragement to its opponents in the Gaza strip, West Bank and Lebanon. If Syria and Lebanon were to make peace with Israel, however, Iran would have lost its two friends in the region (Syria's President Assad and the Lebanese Shia extremist group Hizbullah). That in turn might encourage the Iranians to conclude that they had done their duty by their brothers (who had ignored their advice) and that their priority henceforth was the Iranian economy.

The future: still misty

In the mid-1990s the outlook for the Middle East was promising but fraught with risks. If the peace process stayed on track (and that was a big if), it should bring a surge of business confidence to the region. That hope was reflected in the unprecedented international conference on business in the Middle East in Casablanca in October 1994. Investment was crucial. It would not only create new jobs and new optimism but also destroy the breeding-ground for Islamic extremists: unemployment and poor living conditions. Expanding economies should mean more tax revenue to be spent on social welfare, education, public health and other aspects of "good governance". But that would require a display of political will that has been seen only rarely outside the oil-rich Gulf states. All too easily, bloody acts of violence and retribution could throw the peace process off the track that has been so carefully laid for it. Weak-willed politicians could drag their feet. Nothing would please the men of violence more. The adoption of extreme negotiating positions could set the process back too. Nonetheless, all the signs were that peace in the Middle East was for the first time within reach.

═══ Part I ═══
COUNTRY RANKINGS

The land and the people

Area *sq km*

1	Saudi Arabia	2,400,900	10	Syria	185,180
2	Algeria	2,381,745	11	Tunisia	163,610
3	Libya	1,759,540	12	Jordan	91,880
4	Iran	1,648,000	13	United Arab Emirates	83,600
5	Egypt	1,001,250	14	Israel	20,770
6	Yemen	527,970	15	Kuwait	17,820
7	Morocco	458,730	16	Qatar	11,000
8	Iraq	438,445	17	Lebanon	10,400
9	Oman	212,460	18	Bahrain	620

Agricultural land *% of total*

1	Tunisia	49	9	Egypt	5
2	Yemen	36		Jordan	5
3	Syria	33	11	Bahrain	4
4	Lebanon	30	12	Algeria	3
5	Israel	22	13	United Arab Emirates	2
6	Morocco	19	14	Saudi Arabia	1
7	Iraq	13		Libya	1
8	Iran	8			

Population *millions*

1	Iran	61.4	10	Israel	5.3
2	Egypt	55.8	11	Libya	4.9
3	Algeria	26.9	12	Jordan	4.3
4	Morocco	26.7	13	Lebanon	2.9
5	Iraq	19.8	14	Kuwait	1.9
6	Saudi Arabia	17.4	15	United Arab Emirates	1.7
7	Syria	13.3	16	Oman	1.6
8	Yemen	12.6	17	Bahrain	0.5
9	Tunisia	8.4		Qatar	0.5

Population *millions, 2010 forecast*

1	Iran	96.0	10	Libya	8.8
2	Egypt	72.7	11	Israel	6.8
3	Algeria	38.4	12	Jordan	6.7
4	Morocco	35.9	13	Lebanon	4.9
5	Iraq	32.5	14	Oman	3.3
6	Saudi Arabia	30.0	15	Kuwait	2.3
7	Yemen	23.6	16	United Arab Emirates	2.3
8	Syria	23.3	17	Bahrain	0.8
9	Tunisia	11.9	18	Qatar	0.7

Population growth *average annual increase 1987–92, %*

1	Qatar	4.9		Jordan	3.1
2	Oman	4.5	11	Saudi Arabia	3.0
3	Libya	4.2	12	Algeria	2.6
4	Syria	3.4	13	Iran	2.4
	United Arab Emirates	3.4		Egypt	2.4
	Bahrain	3.4		Kuwait	2.4
7	Yemen	3.3	16	Morocco	2.2
8	Israel	3.2	17	Tunisia	1.9
9	Iraq	3.1	18	Lebanon	0.8

Population growth *av. ann. incr. 1995–2010, %, forecast*

1	Oman	3.8	10	Algeria	2.1
2	Yemen	3.4	11	Bahrain	2.0
3	Libya	3.3	12	United Arab Emirates	1.8
	Syria	3.3		Tunisia	1.8
5	Saudi Arabia	3.2	14	Morocco	1.7
6	Iraq	3.0	15	Qatar	1.6
7	Jordan	2.8		Egypt	1.6
8	Iran	2.7	17	Lebanon	1.4
9	Kuwait	2.4	18	Israel	1.3

Population density *population per sq km*

1	Bahrain	533	10	Iraq	45
2	Lebanon	286	11	Qatar	41
3	Israel	255	12	Iran	37
4	Kuwait	107	13	Yemen	24
5	Syria	72	14	United Arab Emirates	20
6	Morocco	59	15	Algeria	11
7	Egypt	56	16	Oman	8
8	Tunisia	51		Saudi Arabia	8
9	Jordan	48	18	Libya	3

Urban population *% of total*

1	Kuwait	96	10	Jordan	69
2	Israel	92	11	Iran	58
3	Lebanon	85	12	Tunisia	57
4	Libya	84	13	Algeria	54
5	Bahrain	83	14	Syria	51
6	United Arab Emirates	82	15	Morocco	47
7	Qatar	79	16	Egypt	44
8	Saudi Arabia	78	17	Yemen	31
9	Iraq	73	18	Oman	12

Living standards

Human development index

1	Israel	90.0	10	Iran		67.2
2	Kuwait	80.9	11	Oman		65.4
3	Qatar	79.5	12	Jordan		62.8
4	Bahrain	79.1	13	Iraq		61.4
5	Saudi Arabia	74.2	14	Lebanon		60.0
6	Syria	72.7	15	Algeria		55.3
7	United Arab Emirates	70.8	16	Egypt		55.1
8	Libya	70.3	17	Morocco		54.9
9	Tunisia	69.0	18	Yemen		32.3

Life expectancy: men *age in years*

1	Israel	75	10	Tunisia	67
2	Kuwait	72		Algeria	67
3	Bahrain	70	12	Lebanon	66
	Saudi Arabia	70		Libya	66
	United Arab Emirates	70	14	Egypt	65
6	Iran	69		Syria	65
	Qatar	69	16	Morocco	62
8	Jordan	68		Iraq	62
	Oman	68	18	Yemen	52

Life expectancy: women *age in years*

1	Israel	79		Libya	71
2	Kuwait	76	11	Iran	70
3	Bahrain	75	12	Tunisia	69
4	United Arab Emirates	74		Syria	69
5	Saudi Arabia	73	14	Algeria	68
6	Qatar	72	15	Egypt	67
	Jordan	72	16	Morocco	65
	Oman	72	17	Iraq	64
9	Lebanon	71	18	Yemen	53

Infant mortality *number of deaths per 1,000 live births*

1	Yemen	106	10	Syria	36
2	Iraq	84	11	Saudi Arabia	28
3	Iran	65	12	Qatar	24
4	Libya	60	13	Bahrain	21
5	Morocco	57	14	United Arab Emirates	20
	Egypt	57		Oman	20
7	Algeria	55	16	Jordan	18
8	Tunisia	48	17	Kuwait	14
9	Lebanon	43	18	Israel	9

Doctors and patients *number of people per doctor*

1	Morocco	4,840		9	Bahrain	930
2	Iran	3,140		10	Jordan	770
3	Algeria	2,330		11	Saudi Arabia	700
4	Tunisia	1,870		12	Libya	690
5	Egypt	1,320			Kuwait	690
6	Syria	1,160		14	Lebanon	670
7	Oman	1,060		15	Qatar	530
8	United Arab Emirates	1,040		16	Israel	410

Literacy *% of population aged over 17*

1	Israel	95.0		10	United Arab Emirates	65.0
2	Jordan	82.1		11	Saudi Arabia	64.1
3	Lebanon	81.3		12	Iraq	62.5
4	Bahrain	79.0		13	Algeria	60.6
5	Qatar	76.0		14	Iran	56.0
6	Kuwait	73.9		15	Morocco	52.5
7	Tunisia	68.1		16	Egypt	50.0
8	Syria	66.6		17	Yemen	41.0
9	Libya	66.5		18	Oman	35.0

Primary school enrolment *% of age group*

1	Tunisia	117		10	Jordan	97
2	United Arab Emirates	115		11	Israel	95
3	Lebanon	112			Algeria	95
	Iran	112		13	Kuwait	92
5	Iraq	111		14	Bahrain	92
6	Syria	109		15	Saudi Arabia	77
7	Qatar	104		16	Yemen	76
8	Egypt	101			Morocco	66
9	Oman	100				

TV ownership *per 100 population*

1	Oman	75.5		10	Libya	9.9
2	Qatar	44.5		11	Tunisia	8.1
3	Bahrain	41.4			Jordan	8.1
4	Lebanon	32.5		13	Morocco	7.4
5	Kuwait	27.1			Algeria	7.4
6	Saudi Arabia	26.9		15	Iraq	7.2
7	Israel	26.0		16	Iran	6.5
8	United Arab Emirates	11.0		17	Syria	6.0
9	Egypt	10.9		18	Yemen	2.9

The economy

GDP $bn

1	Saudi Arabia	121.0	10	Yemen	22.6
2	Israel	72.7	11	Iraq	18.0
3	Iran	47.0	12	Syria	16.2
4	Algeria	44.0	13	Tunisia	15.3
5	United Arab Emirates	38.7	14	Oman	9.6
6	Egypt	36.7	15	Qatar	7.9
7	Kuwait	34.1	16	Jordan	4.9
8	Morocco	27.6	17	Bahrain	4.5
9	Libya	23.5	18	Lebanon	4.0

GDP per head $

1	Kuwait	23,350	10	Algeria	1,650
2	United Arab Emirates	22,470	11	Lebanon	1,363
3	Qatar	15,140	12	Syria	1,210
4	Israel	13,760	13	Jordan	1,190
5	Bahrain	8,309	14	Yemen	1,089
6	Saudi Arabia	6,958	15	Morocco	1,030
7	Oman	5,600	16	Iraq	911
8	Libya	4,682	17	Iran	765
9	Tunisia	1,780	18	Egypt	660

Purchasing power *GDP per head in PPP, international $*

1	United Arab Emirates	23,390	6	Tunisia	5,070
2	Qatar	22,910	7	Algeria	4,390
3	Israel	14,890	8	Jordan	4,010
4	Bahrain	13,480	9	Egypt	3,530
5	Oman	10,720	10	Morocco	3,270

Agricultural output *as % of GDP*

1	Syria	30.0	10	Saudi Arabia	7.3
2	Yemen	21.0	11	Iraq	5.1
3	Iran[a]	17.8	12	Libya[a]	4.5
4	Tunisia	16.2	13	Oman[a]	4.0
5	Egypt[b]	15.6	14	Israel	2.4
6	Morocco	14.3	15	United Arab Emirates	2.0
7	Lebanon[a]	12.6	16	Bahrain[b]	1.1
8	Algeria	12.0	17	Qatar[a]	1.0
9	Jordan	8.0	18	Kuwait[a]	0.0

Aid received $m

1	Egypt	4,300	10	Lebanon	208
2	Israel	1,434	11	Iraq	158
3	Morocco	758	12	Oman	112
4	Syria	520	13	Saudi Arabia	19
5	Iran	488	14	Bahrain	13
6	Jordan	417	15	Libya	6
7	Tunisia	325	16	United Arab Emirates	4
8	Algeria	318	17	Kuwait	3
9	Yemen	220	18	Qatar	2

Foreign debt $m

1	Iraq	82,884	9	Saudi Arabia	19,496
2	Egypt	40,626	10	United Arab Emirates	11,070
3	Israel	26,481	11	Tunisia	8,701
4	Algeria	25,757	12	Jordan	6,972
5	Kuwait	21,915	13	Yemen	5,923
6	Morocco	21,430	14	Libya	5,733
7	Iran	20,550	15	Oman	2,661
8	Syria	19,975	16	Lebanon	1,356

Foreign debt as % of GDP

1	Iraq	460.1	9	Yemen	56.4
2	Jordan	142.9	10	Israel	40.7
3	Syria	122.8	11	Oman	34.9
4	Egypt	104.8	12	United Arab Emirates	30.9
5	Morocco	81.7	13	Libya	24.3
6	Kuwait	74.6	14	Lebanon	16.9
7	Tunisia	59.9	14	Saudi Arabia	16.0
8	Algeria	57.4			

Debt service due $m

1	Algeria	9,110	9	Syria	1,336
2	Egypt	4,749	10	Tunisia	1,283
3	Israel	3,182	11	United Arab Emirates	1,278
4	Morocco	2,658	12	Libya	858
5	Saudi Arabia	2,370	13	Oman	583
6	Jordan	1,747	14	Yemen	525
7	Iran	1,612	15	Lebanon	67
8	Kuwait	1,577			

Debt service ratio

1	Algeria	76.9	8	Kuwait	9.0
2	Morocco	30.7	9	Yemen	7.5
3	Tunisia	20.2	10	Iran	7.2
4	Egypt	15.2	11	United Arab Emirates	6.5
5	Jordan	14.6	12	Lebanon	6.5
6	Israel	14.4	13	Syria	5.3
7	Libya	10.1	14	Saudi Arabia	4.5

Aid received per head

1	Israel	280	10	Yemen	18
2	Jordan	89	11	Algeria	12
3	Egypt	78	12	Iran	9
4	Lebanon	77	13	Iraq	8
5	Oman	58	14	Qatar	4
6	Syria	40	15	United Arab Emirates	2
7	Tunisia	39		Kuwait	2
8	Morocco	30	17	Saudi Arabia	1
9	Bahrain	26		Libya	1

a 1992. b 1988.

=Part II=
COUNTRY PROFILES

ALGERIA

Total area	2,381,745 sq km	Population	26.9m
GDP	$44.0bn	GDP per head	$1,650
Capital	Algiers	Other cities	Oran, Constantine

"Too little, too late" may be the verdict on Algeria's military rulers in their bid to prevent a takeover of the government by violent Islamic fundamentalists. For years this relatively sophisticated Arab country, with its strong French influence, was allowed to stagnate under the dead hand of a military-backed socialist state. An attempt at reform began to improve it. But too many of the unemployed, the alienated and the insecure had found solace in an extreme version of Islam. By 1995 the violence had become almost endemic.

History: rebellious

Arab culture and Islam came to the predominantly Berber peoples of what is now Algeria in the 7th century and survived subsequent invasions. Among them was the arrival of the Turks in the 16th century, when Ottoman proconsuls ruled Mediterranean towns including Algiers. The Berbers kept control of the interior. The Turks were followed by the French, who came in 1830 and stayed until 1962. Algeria became part of Metropolitan France. In the 1830s and 1840s a skilful rebel leader, Abdul Kadir, led some of the Berbers against the invaders, but was defeated in 1847. By 1870 French settlers had grabbed most of the country's best land. The Algerians, dispossessed and bitter, staged an unsuccessful revolt in 1871. Nationalism grew.

France retreated

When allied forces landed in North Africa in 1942 a nationalist leader, Ferhat Abbas, demanded a post-war constituent assembly and universal suffrage. Five years later France gave French citizenship to all Algerians and set up a two-chamber assembly, one for the French and the other for the Algerians. But the voting was rigged. Rebellion was inevitable. The National Liberation Front (FLN) launched a guerrilla war in 1956 with bomb attacks; the French responded with repression and torture. It was a time of terror and hatred. The settlers, determined not to let power pass to the Algerians, staged revolts of their own and formed the notorious Secret Army Organisation, which was said to have killed, tortured and intimidated many Algerians. The settlers hoped that General de Gaulle, who came to power in 1958, would be on their side. But the shrewd de Gaulle knew when he was beaten. In 1962 France made an agreement with the FLN at Evian paving the way for independence on July 5th.

Internal divisions

A scramble for power followed in which Ahmed Ben Bella emerged as leader and other long-standing chiefs such as Muhammad Boudiaf went into opposition or exile. Ben Bella held power only until 1965 when a dour army commander, Houari Boumedienne, seized control. Boumedienne launched Algeria on the road to socialism in a one-party state. He nationalised many private companies. The successor state enterprises were too protected and too inefficient; they sank into a bureaucratic quagmire. Algeria was well on the way to stagflation when Boumedienne died in 1978. His successor, General Chadli Benjedid, spent two years consolidating his power and then began gingerly to free the economy. He encouraged private enterprise but did not try to privatise the big state companies. He allowed opposition parties to form. But trouble loomed. Unemployment in a country with little private enterprise was rising. In 1988 strikes led to rioting in Algiers and other cities in which hundreds were killed. This was a stimulus to the Islamic Salvation Front (FIS). At this point Algeria began to crumble.

The rise of the Islamists

President Chadli allowed Algeria's first multi-party elections, for local governments, to be held in 1990. The FIS beat the ruling FLN and FIS militants began bullying westernised Algerians. Nonetheless, the president persisted and ordered a parliamentary election in two stages on December 26th 1991 and January 16th 1992. In the first round the FIS won 55.4% of the vote and was set to win a clear parliamentary majority in the second. President Chadli suddenly resigned on January 11th and was replaced by a military-backed Higher State Council led by an old exiled rebel, Muhammad Boudiaf. It suspended the second round. Boudiaf was assassinated in June. The appointment in January 1994 of General Liamine Zeroual as president, replacing the Higher State Council, did not bring political stability.

Politics: a search for interlocutors

In 1994 Muslim fundamentalists were murdering Europeans (most of whom had fled the country), women going unveiled in public, army officers, police, non-religious intellectuals, artists and journalists. By the middle of the year some 4,000 Algerians and at least 37 foreigners had been killed. President Zeroual said he could see only a negotiated settlement and tried to do a deal with jailed FIS leaders. The FIS stated its terms: recognition as a political party; release of political prisoners; and a commitment to democracy. General Zeroual appointed a six-member group including ex-President Ben Bella to try to negotiate. Against such a settlement (which could easily lead to a FIS victory at the polls and the "Islamisation" of Algeria) was the hardline chief of staff, Major-General Muhammad Lamari.

Meeting in Rome

In January 1995 almost all the opposition groups including two representatives of the FIS met in Rome. They pledged themselves to abide by the rules: free multi-party elections and peaceful transfers of power, freedom of association and of the press. General Zeroual, who had gained a reputation for being a conciliator, turned them down, possibly under pressure from hardliners who wanted to eradicate the FIS. He insisted he would hold a presidential election, but not a parliamentary one, by the end of 1995. That was unacceptable to much of the opposition.

Foreign policy: trying to be helpful, sometimes

Under Boumedienne, Algeria tried to become a leader of the third world at meetings of the Non-Aligned Movement and a mediator in international disputes. The Chadli government was more concerned with the economic mess at home. Nonetheless, it played a key role in solving the crisis over the American embassy hostages in Tehran. Negotiations in 1981 were completed in Algiers. Under Boumedienne, who posed as an Arab radical, Algeria's relations with conservative Morocco were bad. This was because it recognised and helped the Polisario guerrillas who laid claim to the former Western Sahara (a territory between Morocco and Mauritania which Spain had ceded to them in equal shares, and Morocco had taken over entirely). Chadli preferred to be on good terms with the influential King Hassan of Morocco.

Society: too many people

Algeria's 26.4m population is expected to grow to 38.4m by 2010. However, the population growth rate has fallen from 3.5% in the 1980s to less than 3%. This welcome development is nonetheless late: the population growth that has occurred already will create a massive influx into the workforce in the next two decades. Family planning is spreading;

its techniques are used by 36% of married women. But Islamic fundamentalists are discouraging them. Unemployment, at about 30% of the workforce, is social dynamite. Only in optimum conditions, with a peaceful democratic settlement of the country's conflict, will it fall. Educational standards are already falling because of the crisis. But adult literacy, quite high by regional standards at 61%, should improve.

The economy: IMF to the rescue?

It is hard to see how a heavily state-controlled economy can give Algeria the boost of confidence it desperately needs. However, with its income from oil and natural gas, Algeria might do better than expected. In 1994 it signed an agreement with the International Monetary Fund for a loan of $375m with the prospect of a bigger one in 1995 in return for promises to liberalise the exchange rate (the dinar was devalued by 40% in April 1994) and to bring inflation below 20% and the budget deficit below 3% of GDP by 1995. If these promises are kept, the government should stabilise the economy and create an atmosphere that might encourage some successful privatisations. Other lending institutions such as the World Bank also offered loans in 1995.

Oil and gas remain the key. The state oil company, Sonatrach, was seeking investments of $17 billion in 1994. Many foreign oil companies were interested in prospecting for and exploiting new deposits. Liquid natural gas production was due to increase from 18m tons in 1992 to 22m tons in 1996 and more thereafter. Fiat, Daewoo and Coca-Cola were investing in Algeria. But for most companies the political risk, and the personal danger, was overwhelming.

Take a chance?

For the daring, Algeria will offer a free-trade zone and a "one-stop" investment agency. A deal could be worked out to exploit a gold mine in the south. Foreign high-street banks are still not wanted but the idea of setting up local privately owned banks was being encouraged. There were plans to promote more joint enterprises. The appointment of an ex-World Bank man to take charge of industrial restructuring was seen as encouraging. Analysts reckoned that if the country could be held together somehow, without any Iranian-style Islamic excesses, and the modest private sector was given a chance to spread its wings, GDP could even start growing by about 3% a year. Optimists were dreaming that such economic growth would help to restore political stability. Pessimists said it was all too late.

Total area	2,381,745 sq km	% agricultural area	3
Capital	Algiers	Highest point metres	Mt Tahat
Other cities	Oran, Constantine,		2,918
	Annaba	Main rivers	Chelif, Nahar, Quassel

The economy

GDP $bn	44.0	GDP per head $	1,650
% av. ann. growth in		GDP per head in purchasing	
real GDP 1985–93	0.3	power parity $	4,390

Origins of GDP	% of total	Components of GDP	% of total
Agriculture	12.0	Private consumption	48.5
Industry	49.3	Public consumption	15.9
of which:		Investment	29.8
manufacturing	10.1	Exports	30.7
Services	17.9	Imports	-25.0

Production *average annual change 1985–93, %*

Agriculture	5.0	Manufacturing	-8.4
Industry	-1.6	Services	0.8

Inflation and exchange rates

Consumer price 1993 av. ann. incr. 20.5%		Dinars per $ av. 1994	35.06
Av. ann. rate 1988–93	20.6%	Dinars per SDR av. 1994	53.68

Balance of payments, reserves, aid and debt $bn

Visible exports fob	12.3	Capital balance	-2.1
Visible imports fob	-6.9	Overall balance	1.0
Trade balance	5.5	Change in reserves	0.4
Invisible inflows	0.5	Level of reserves end Dec.	1.7
Invisible outflows	-3.8	Foreign debt	25.7
Net transfers	0.2	as % of GDP	57.4
Current account balance	2.4	Debt service	9.1
as % of GDP	4.5	as % of export earnings	76.9

Principal exports*	$bn fob	Principal imports*	$bn cif
Energy & lubricants	10.9	Capital goods	3.7
		Food	2.1
		Semi-finished products	1.8
		Consumer goods	1.1
Total	11.1	Total	9.5

Main export destinations	% of total	Main origins of imports	% of total
Italy	17.2	France	29.9
United States	15.2	United States	12.7
Germany	12.6	Italy	11.9
France	12.1	Spain	11.1
Netherlands	7.3	Germany	5.3
Spain	7.0	Japan	3.5

Government
System Republic with unicameral National People's Assembly. Executive branch composed of president, prime minister and council of ministers.
Main political parties Islamic Salvation Front (FIS), National Liberation Front (FLN), Socialist Forces Front (FFS)

Climate and topography
Arid to semi-arid. Mild wet winters with hot dry summers along the coast. Drier with greater extremes in the interior. Narrow, discontinuous coastal plain. Interior mostly high plateau and desert with some mountains.

People and society

Population m	26.9	% under 15	41.3
Pop. per sq km	11	% over 65	3.4
% urban	54	No. men per 100 women	100
% av. ann. growth 1987–92	2.6	Human Development Index	55.3
No. households m	…		

Life expectancy		Education	
Men	68 yrs	Spending as % of GDP	5.6
Women	70 yrs	Mean years of schooling	2.8
Crude birth rate	27	Adult literacy %	60.6
Crude death rate	6	Primary school enrolment %	95
Infant mortality rate	55	Secondary school enrolment %	60
Under-5 mortality rate	80	Tertiary education enrolment %	12

Workforce	% of total	Consumer goods ownership	
Services	49	Telephone mainlines per 1,000	32
Industry	33	Televisions per 100	7.4
Agriculture	18		
% of total population	24		

Ethnic groups	% of total	Religious groups	% of total
Arab-Berber	99	Sunni Muslim	99
European	1	Christian & Jewish	1

Tourism		Health	
Tourist receipts $m	75	Pop. per doctor	2,330
		Low birthweight babies % of total	9
		Daily calories % of total requirement	118
		% pop. with access to safe water	70

a 1991.
b 1990.

BAHRAIN

Total area	620 sq km	Population	508,000
GDP	$4.5bn	GDP per head	$8,309
Capital	Manama	Other cities	Muharraq, Jidhafs

Under the firm rule of the shrewd al-Khalifa family, Bahrain has developed a diversified economy that is not over-dependent on oil and is increasingly open. The island has avoided potential trouble from its sensitive Shia-Sunni split among Muslims and from some of its more difficult neighbours. Over the long term, Bahrain faces a more serious challenge: to create enough new jobs to employ the ever-growing population. The prospects for democracy, on the other hand, are dim.

History: the British period

Bahrain is a relatively small island in an archipelago of 35 largely barren islands on the Gulf coast sandwiched between Qatar, to the east, and Saudi Arabia, to the west, to which it is linked by a heavily used 25km causeway built for $900m in 1986. The Portuguese ruled the area in the 16th century and the Iranians in the 17th and 18th. Iran was expelled by the tribe led by the al-Khalifa family and has never forgotten this reverse. The al-Khalifas have mostly been in charge since 1783.

Britain, ever anxious to keep other European powers out of what it saw as the approaches to British India, kept a close eye on the Gulf in the 19th century. Germany, France and Russia as well as Iran and Turkey wanted to move in for different reasons. Aware of Bahrain's vulnerability and the strength of Britain in the region, the al-Khalifas signed agreements for what amounted to a protectorate with the British in 1861, 1880 and 1892. Increasingly Britain administered the islands.

All that changed when Britain decided to withdraw from the Gulf by the end of 1971. In 1968 Bahrain said it would join what was then called the federation of Arab emirates. Closer examination of the way the federation was to be run, and of the different level of economic and social development of the southern sheikhdoms compared with Bahrain's, persuaded the ruler, Sheikh Isa bin Sulman al-Khalifa, to go for independence instead. Bahrain became independent in 1971. Isa took the title of amir. In 1981 Bahrain joined the Gulf Co-operation Council, comprising Saudi Arabia, Oman, Kuwait, the United Arab Emirates and Qatar as well as Bahrain.

Politics: powerless assemblies

The first elections were held in 1972 when male Bahraini voters elected 22 members of a constituent assembly. A constitution emerged the following year, when elections were held for 30 members of a 44-member National Assembly (the remaining seats were to be held by cabinet ministers). This lasted until 1975 when Sheikh Khalifa, annoyed that the assembly had come into conflict with the government, dissolved it and suspended the constitution. It was only in 1992 that he appointed a 30-member Consultative Council, made up mostly of businessmen plus some lawyers, judges and former assemblymen. The council can question cabinet ministers and comment on draft laws, but it cannot legislate. That is the sheikh's job. The council's meetings are not open to the news media (unlike Oman's) or to the public, and are not reported on fully. Eight of the 16 cabinet ministers in 1994 came from the Khalifa family. There appeared to be no prospect of a democratic opening.

A delicate matter

There are at least two reasons why Bahrain's rulers do not wish to share power with elected representatives of the people. One is that life is more pleasant for them if they are answerable to no one. The other is that Bahrain has a sensitive religious difficulty. About 70% of the population is Shia Muslim. The remaining 30%, including the al-Khalifa family, is Sunni. With Shia Muslim Iran just across the Gulf and enthusiastic about spreading its gospel, this is a problem. Iran also has a claim on Bahrain based on Iran's occupation of the islands in the 17th and 18th centuries. The shah of Iran appeared to have dropped this claim in 1970 following publication of a UN report. But Ayatollah Khomeini's revolutionary government revived it in 1979, and Bahrain suspected it of trouble-making among the islands' Shia population. The Bahraini government has been vigilant. A 1993 report by Amnesty International cited countless reports of Bahraini Shia who had been stripped of their nationality and expelled to neighbouring countries.

Grenades in the mosque

In a sign of the times in January 1994 at least 20 people were arrested at a mosque in Manama where Shia Muslims had gathered to mourn the death of a revered Shia ayatollah in Iran. Police sealed off the mosque and fired tear-gas grenades into its compound. Police said the demonstration, attended by "hundreds" of people; was unauthorised. In a move that may have been a gesture of reconciliation, the amir was said to have pardoned a number of Bahrainis who had been in exile since the 1980s for "breaking the law".

Foreign policy: islands and alliances

Bahrain depends considerably on neighbouring Saudi Arabia which, along with Kuwait, gives financial support to the island government. The last thing the Saudis want is for Bahrain to be taken over by a pro-Iranian radical Shia Muslim regime. Nonetheless, regardless of its concern over its Shia Muslims, Bahrain was solidly behind Saudi Arabia in its support for Iraq against Iran in the 1980–88 war. Bahrain's relations with Iran slumped. Its rulers suspected that Iran was behind what they described as an unsuccessful coup attempt. Relations with Iran were restored in 1990 after Bahrain opposed Iraq's occupation of Kuwait.

A little local difficulty

In 1986 a long-standing dispute with neighbouring Qatar erupted. Both claimed the Hawar islands, off Qatar's west coast, plus some reefs. What mattered was not the islands but what might lie under them. Qatar invaded the man-made island of Fasht al-Dibal and seized some foreign workers contracted by Bahrain to reclaim the site from the sea. With Saudi mediation the workers were freed and the island destroyed. That was not the end of it, however. In 1991 Qatar took its claim to the World Court in The Hague; Bahrain contested the court's jurisdiction. After further Saudi mediation, the dispute has apparently been buried at least temporarily.

Society: well-educated

Bahrainis are relatively well educated with 20% having completed some form of secondary education. The number of state schools, 139 in 1986, has been increasing since the end of the Gulf war. There is an Arab Gulf University at Sakhir and a Gulf Technical College. The shipyard and the banks do their own training. A pension scheme for Bahraini nationals has been launched. It is deducted from salaries: employees pay 7%, employers 11%.

The economy: explosive unemployment

The number of people unemployed is small because Bahrain and its outer islands are small. But the potential increase in unemployment still represents social dynamite. For example, the number of Bahrainis under the age of 25, in a population of 508,000, is expected to have increased by 60,000 in the year 2000. The number of graduates will increase by 44,000 over the same period. How many jobs will be available for them? By one rough calculation 3,000 young people enter the labour market every year and there are only about 1,000 jobs for them. There is one easy tactic which the government has already tried: expelling expatriate workers who do not have work permits. At least 300 were expelled in 1993. Nonetheless, some 38% of the workforce are expatriates.

Not enough oil

Bahrain's difficulties will worsen: its oil reserves are fast dwindling and may run out early in the next century. Oil production is slipping, but production of natural gas is on the increase. As part of its diversification programme, the government is planning to launch a new port and free-trade zone at Hidd. The idea of the Portuguese planners is to have a port with a capacity of 600,000 containers. The courier company DHL has been encouraged to open a regional base at Bahrain airport. Gulf Air, the regional airline controlled by Bahrain, Qatar, Abu Dhabi and Oman, is to be privatised. The government is also encouraging small and medium-sized businesses: they are given cash payments for every additional employee they take on. The government's liberalisation of the rules governing foreign investment, allowing the establishment of foreign-owned companies, is producing results: Bahrain registered 32 companies in 1992, 42 in 1993 and about 100 in 1994.

Looking around

A relatively unexplored market for diversification is tourism. More than 500,000 visitors stayed at local hotels in 1993 for the equivalent of over 1m room-nights. The government wants to do better and the Bahrain Leisure Company has been launched to promote the industry. An aluminium smelter owned by ALBA was a victim of the whims of the world price, but the Gulf Aluminium Rolling Mill company was investing in an American rolling mill. The government hoped banking would develop a services industry in Bahrain rather like that of Dubai. A stock exchange was opened in 1989. But the outlook for Bahrain is fuzzy. When the oil runs out it will be weak. The chances are that Saudi Arabia, which has a mainly Shia Muslim population living near Bahrain and worries constantly about it, will come to Bahrain's rescue. That is a fate the al-Khalifas want to avoid. It is why they are racing to diversify the economy.

Total area	620 sq km	% agricultural area	4
Capital	Manama	Highest point metres	Jabal ad-
Other cities	Muharraq, Jidhafs		Dukhan 135

The economy

GDP $bn	4.5	GDP per head $	8,309
% av. ann. growth in		GDP per head in purchasing	
real GDP 1985–93	2.3	power parity $	13,480

Origins of GDP[a]	% of total	Components of GDP	% of total
Agriculture	1.1	Private consumption	32.8
Industry	36.3	Public consumption	23.6
of which:		Investment	25.0
manufacturing	62.6	Exports	108.5
Services	...	Imports	-93.4

Production average annual change 1985–93, %

Agriculture	...	Manufacturing	...
Industry	...	Services	...

Inflation and exchange rates

Consumer price 1993 av. ann. incr.	2.0%	Dinars per $ av. 1994	0.38
Av. ann. rate 1988–93	1.0%	Dinars per SDR av. 1994	0.54

Balance of payments, reserves, aid and debt

			$bn
Visible exports fob	3.7	Capital balance	0.4
Visible imports fob	-3.8	Overall balance	-0.08
Trade balance	-0.1	Change in reserves	-0.1
Invisible inflows	1.3	Level of reserves end Dec.	1.3
Invisible outflows	-1.7	Foreign debt	2.6
Net transfers	-0.07	as % of GDP	57.6
Current account balance	-0.6	Debt service	0.3
as % of GDP	-13.9	as % of export earnings	5.9

Principal exports[b]	$m fob	Principal imports[b]	$m cif
Petroleum products	2,605	Mineral fuels	1,553
Manufactures	672	Machinery & transport equip.	1,077
		Manufactures	787
		Chemicals	289
Total	3,417	Total	4,145

Main export destinations	% of total	Main origins of imports	% of total
Japan	11.4	Saudi Arabia	46.7
UAE	4.7	United Kingdom	6.8
South Korea	4.1	Japan	6.7
India	3.6	United States	6.1
Saudi Arabia	3.4	Germany	4.6

Government

System Monarchy. Constitution ratified in June 1973. Provides for a unicameral National Assembly, which was dissolved in August 1975. Legislative powers were assumed by the Cabinet, which is appointed by the amir.

Main political parties None

Climate and topography

Mild winters, very hot, humid summers. Mostly low desert plain rising gently to a low central escarpment.

People and society

Population m	0.5	% under 15	35.6
Pop. per sq km	533	% over 65	2.4
% urban	83	No. men per 100 women	135
% av. ann. growth 1987–92	3.4	Human Development Index	79.1
No. households m	...		

Life expectancy		**Education**	
Men	70 yrs	Spending as % of GDP	...
Women	75 yrs	Mean years of schooling	4.3
Crude birth rate	27	Adult literacy %	79
Crude death rate	4	Primary school enrolment %	92
Infant mortality rate	21	Secondary school enrolment %	95
Under-5 mortality rate	15	Tertiary education enrolment %	18

Workforce	% of total	**Consumer goods ownership**	
Services	83	Telephone mainlines per 1,000	...
Industry	14	Televisions per 100	41.4
Agriculture	3		
% of total population	45		

Ethnic groups	% of total	**Religious groups**	% of total
Bahraini	63	Shia Muslim	70
Asian	13	Sunni Muslim	30
Other Arab	10		

Tourism		**Health**	
Tourist receipts $m	177	Pop. per doctor	930
		Low birthweight babies % of total	...
		Daily calories % of total requirement	...
		% pop. with access to safe water	100

a 1988.
b 1992.

EGYPT

Total area	1,001,250 sq km	Population	55.8m
GDP	$36.7bn	GDP per head	$660
Capital	Cairo	Other cities	Alexandria, Giza

Badly managed, over-populated, under-developed and messy, Egypt is nonetheless the heart of the Arab world. Some Arab countries are richer. Some have more efficient governments. But few have deeper cultural roots, longer traditions, older universities and a greater sense of regional leadership. Under President Hosni Mubarak that leadership has been exercised through vigorous and skilful diplomacy.

History: Alexander and Cleopatra

From the end of the fourth millenium BC until conquest by the Assyrians in 671BC, Egypt was ruled by the pharaohs. They built the pyramids in the third millenium. The Assyrians were succeeded by the Persians, who gave way to Alexander the Great in 332BC. Alexander was succeeded by his general, Ptolemy, whose dynasty introduced Egyptian culture to aspects of Greek civilisation. The Coptic church was founded. When Cleopatra died in 30BC, the Romans took over, and stayed until ousted by Arab armies in an invasion that was completed by 641AD. Egypt was subsequently ruled by various dynasties until the Turks took over in 1517 and made it part of the Ottoman empire. Curiously, some western influences were introduced by Muhammad Ali, an Ottoman army officer who seized power in 1807. Under his son, Said Pasha, construction of the Suez Canal began. It was opened in 1869 and French and British influence spread. In 1882 the British invaded and defeated Egyptian forces at Tel el-Kebir. Egypt remained in name an Ottoman province until the outbreak of the first world war. But when Turkey sided with Germany the British took over and it became a protectorate. In 1922 the British granted independence of a sort; they retained the right to defend the canal and Egypt itself (and to keep troops there). They agreed to withdraw their troops to the Suez Canal Zone 14 years later.

A bold move

The establishment of the state of Israel in 1948, coupled with corruption in the Egyptian monarchy and British dominance, stirred nationalism in Cairo. In 1952 a group of army officers ousted King Farouk and replaced him with General Muhammad Neguib. Two years later a stormy new leader took over: Gamal Abdel Nasser, apostle of pan-Arab nationalism, state socialism, land reform, social welfare, a pro-Soviet but officially non-aligned foreign policy and national-isation of the Suez Canal Company. Nasser, who became a strongman, took over the canal in 1956. He said he would use canal dues to pay for the construction of the Aswan dam on the Nile, which Britain and the United States had refused to finance. All this provoked an invasion by Britain and France in cahoots with Israel that was fiercely opposed by the United States under President Eisenhower. American pressure obliged the three invading forces to withdraw. Nasser kept control of the canal, which reopened in 1957, and he became an Egyptian hero. Three years later he united Egypt with Syria: the marriage did not last.

A rash action

Nasser's confrontation with Israel in 1967 was foolhardy and disastrous. He ordered the dissolution of the UN force based on the Egyptian side of the border with Israel and, by seizing Sharm el-Sheikh at the entrance to the Gulf of Aqaba, made it impossible for the Israelis to use their Gulf port, Eilat. It was an act of war. On June 5th 1967 Israel air-craft destroyed Egypt's air force in a matter of hours. The army swiftly seized east Jerusalem and the West Bank from Jordan, the Sinai desert up to the Suez Canal from Egypt and the Golan Heights from Syria. The Suez Canal was closed. It was all over in an extraordinary six days. Egypt, humiliated, ran out of cash and had to beg from Saudi Ara-bia, Kuwait, Libya and the Soviet Union, which had been arming and training the Egyptian armed forces. State social-ism was not providing enough jobs. Political dissent grew.

A brave man

Nasser was succeeded on his death in 1970 by his vice-president, Anwar Sadat, who changed the history of the Mid-dle East. First, he ordered the withdrawal of hundreds of Soviet military advisers based at Alexandria in 1972 and turned instead to the United States as his main ally and aid-giver. Second, he made peace with Israel. Sadat knew that in order to have a respectable negotiating position with Israel he would first have to break the stalemate and score a partial military victory. He did this with his surprise invasion of Israel in October 1973 during Israel's religious celebration of Yom Kippur. Before the fighting stopped, Egyptian forces had crossed the Suez Canal and advanced into the Sinai desert while Israeli forces had crossed the canal and advanced towards southern Egypt, encircling the third Egyptian army. Since both sides appeared to have suffered reverses, the

Egyptians felt they had emerged with honour; Sadat's domestic position was enhanced.

Subsequent negotiations, in which Henry Kissinger's "shuttle diplomacy" played a key role, led to disengagement agreements in the Sinai. Sadat boldly went one step further in 1977 by visiting Israel and addressing its parliament. He offered no concessions and insisted on the restitution of all lands seized by Israel. But he paved the way for the Camp David negotiations a year later that established peace between Egypt and Israel and the framework for negotiations on the future of the Israeli-occupied territories. This was popular at home but rejected as treason by other Arab governments. Egypt was expelled from the Arab League and isolated. Nonetheless, by 1982 Israel had withdrawn from the Sinai desert. It was a remarkable achievement. Sadat was assassinated by an Islamist in 1981.

A minor key

Sadat's successor, his vice-president Hosni Mubarak, lacks his theatrical flair and his taste for palaces and good living. Mr Mubarak is a canny strategist. He adopted a two-track policy of ending Egypt's isolation in the Arab world while maintaining diplomatic relations with Israel correctly but coolly. The policy worked: Egypt was readmitted to the Arab League in 1987; two years later an Egyptian was appointed as the league's secretary-general and its headquarters was moved back to Cairo from Tunis. Eventually, Mr Mubarak became the busiest fixer of meetings between Arab and Israeli leaders. In 1994 the agreement for Israel to hand over the Gaza Strip and Jericho to the Palestine Liberation Organisation was signed in Cairo before the world's media, and the American secretary of state and the Russian foreign minister.

Politics: fear of extremists

In domestic politics, Mr Mubarak wants to ensure the country's stability in order to promote the shaky economy. This has meant cracking down on small bands of violent Islamic fundamentalists which have targeted senior officials, policemen, Copts and foreign tourists. There are two main factions: the Islamic Group (Gamaat Islamiya) and Holy War (Jihad). They are recruited from young men in the lower or lower-middle class who have grown up in the slums of Cairo and the poor towns and villages of Upper (southern) Egypt. Poverty and unemployment are the best recruiters. The Islamic Group operates south of Cairo in towns including Asyut, Minya and Sohag. It has much less influence in Cairo itself and the Nile delta cities (in the north). The second extremist group, Holy War, organised the assassination of Sadat. It operates on an international level. Some of its militants may have been trained in Pakistan and Afghanistan. Holy War killed the speaker of parliament in 1990, a well-known writer in 1992 and the head of the security forces' anti-Islamist section, General Muhammad Khairat, in 1994. But its attempts to kill the information and interior ministers failed. For their part, the police killed the Islamic Group's military commander, Talaat Himam, in 1994. Attacks on tourists appeared to be fading (but receipts from tourism fell by 36% in 1993 and remained depressed in 1994).

All Muslims together

One of the government's tactics has been to broadcast many radio sermons that combine being devout with supporting the government and rejecting violence. This has gone down badly with Cairo liberals who would like fewer sermons. More democracy might help. Mr Mubarak was unconvincingly but overwhelmingly re-elected to a third six-year term in 1993. The 454-seat People's Assembly is the legislature but is widely regarded as a rubber stamp. There is also an advisory council. The president's decrees are law. In the 1984 parliamentary election, the ruling National Democratic Party (NDP) won 389 seats to the combined opposition's 59. In another election three years later, the NDP won 346 seats and the opposition 96. The election was marred by hundreds of arrests and charges of fraud. It was much the same in 1990 (348 to 83) but several opposition parties boycotted the polls.

Too many parties

Thirteen legal parties, mainly in the opposition, were recognised during this period. Most were unimpressive. They did not give Mr Mubarak a serious challenge. The main opposition party was the New Wafd, which has in the past allied with the banned but tolerated Muslim Brotherhood. It has turned conservative and is a strong supporter of the private sector. The second opposition grouping is that of the Socialist Labour Party and the Liberal Socialist Party. The former, despite its name, sounds increasingly Islamist: one of its slogans is "Islam is the answer". In May 1994 Mr Mubarak inaugurated "national dialogue" meetings. There were no places for the Muslim Brotherhood, which had become a target for government denunciations of links to terrorists, or the Islamists. Some party and union leaders and other well-known personalities took part but the Wafd and the

Nasserist Arab Democratic Party boycotted it, claiming the whole affair had been rigged by the NDP. The only concession to the official opposition was a promise that candidates in the 1995 general election could stand on a party ticket and would no longer have to stand as individuals, as required by the Supreme Constitutional Court after the previous election. To please the left there was also an affirmation of the role of the state in redistributing wealth.

Foreign policy: looking west

Sadat's foreign policy was continued by President Mubarak. As a result Egypt received more American aid than any country except Israel. Egypt tried to play an influential role in the Organisation of African Unity as well as the Arab League. Its relations with Libya have been strained and on one occasion almost led to armed conflict, mainly because of the unpredictability of Colonel Muammar Qaddafi. Relations with Sudan were strained because of intelligence reports that Sudan permitted the training of Egyptian Islamist extremists in camps on its territory. Syria, which regards itself as a rival for leadership of the Middle East, treats Egypt coolly. Saudi Arabia, which regards itself as the main Arab country in the Gulf, welcomed the arrival of Egyptian troops during the Gulf war, but is also cool about the idea of Egypt's influence spreading.

Society: too many people, too few jobs

Egypt's population shot up from 33m in 1976 to 54.9m in 1992 and is expected to rise to 72.7m by 2010. Family-planning programmes had reduced the growth rate from 3% in 1985 to a still-high 2.3% in 1993. But early marriages, ignorance of birth-control methods, the lack of jobs for women and poor education in general have not helped. Some Muslim clerics have preached against birth control although the Grand Mufti is in favour. A UN conference on the world's rising population was held in Cairo in 1994. Only half of the 3.2m children entitled to secondary-school education get it. Of the population aged ten or older, 50% are illiterate. Though appalling, this is much better than the 70% in 1960. Relations between the Muslim majority (94% of the population) and the Coptic Christian minority (6%) have usually been trouble-free although fundamentalists have occasionally targeted the Copts. Boutros Boutros-Ghali, who was a deputy prime minister before becoming UN secretary-general, is one of Egypt's leading Copts.

The economy: a delicate balance

President Mubarak has had to steer a careful course on economic policy between demands for social justice, food subsidies and other aspects of the welfare state (which Egypt can ill afford) and insistent requests from the IMF, World Bank and American aid-givers for structural reforms including a balanced budget and, if possible, a trade surplus. Mr Mubarak knows that if he abolishes some subsidies he would have a riot on his hands. Sadat began to dismantle the huge public sector created by Nasser and some bits, notably the tourism industry, have been privatised. But the bigger state enterprises have not.

Egypt is still afflicted by inflation, a shortage of foreign exchange and a large foreign debt. Mr Mubarak started an economic reform programme backed by the IMF in 1991. The idea was to move the country towards a market economy. Industries were removed from the authority of various ministries and placed in supposedly profit-oriented holding companies, 25 of which were meant to be sold off by 1997. Currency controls have been lifted. In the early 1990s the country was running current-account surpluses. But the foreign debt of $40 billion is still too high. Nonetheless, inflation was running in 1994 at a modest 7–8%. High import tariffs were being cut. GDP growth in 1994 was reckoned to be 3%. It was respectable, but not enough to cut high unemployment.

New difficulties

The growing population is taking over farmland for homes and, although the country has a free-market agricultural policy and busily reclaims land from the desert, it has to import half its food needs. For millenia until the Aswan dam was built, the annual flooding of the Nile replenished farms in the delta with rich deposits of silt. The Aswan dam stopped the flood and increased demand for fertiliser, some of it imported. Egypt does export agricultural products. Rice is the biggest followed by cotton, which has been declining for many years, partly owing to low government prices. Animal traction is still vital: in 1990 Egypt had 1.98m donkeys, 190,000 camels and 2.5m buffaloes. Egypt exports oil but output has been static for years, because of a lack of incentives to international oil companies from the state-owned Egyptian General Petroleum Company. For all its faults, Egypt is modernising itself, but not quickly enough. Its economic policymakers should never forget the swelling numbers in the workplace.

Total area	1,001,250 sq km	% agricultural area	5
Capital	Cairo	Highest point metres	Mt Katherina
Other cities	Alexandria, Giza		2,642
		Main rivers	Nile

The economy

GDP $bn	36.7	GDP per head $	660
% av. ann. growth in		GDP per head in purchasing	
real GDP 1985–93	3.0	power parity $	3,530

Origins of GDP[a]	% of total	Components of GDP	% of total
Agriculture	15.6	Private consumption	73.9
Industry	32.9	Public consumption	10.8
of which:		Investment	18.6
manufacturing	...	Exports	28.9
Services	50.5	Imports	-32.2

Production average annual change 1985–93, %

Agriculture	-3.1	Manufacturing	-3.1
Industry	-1.7	Services	-3.9

Inflation and exchange rates

Consumer price 1993 av. ann. incr.	12.1%	Pounds per $ av. 1994	3.39
Av. ann. rate 1988–93	16.7%	Pounds per SDR av. 1994	4.90

Balance of payments, reserves, aid and debt $bn

Visible exports fob	3.2	Capital balance	-1.5
Visible imports fob	-9.9	Overall balance	2.8
Trade balance	-6.7	Change in reserves	2.1
Invisible inflows	9.3	Level of reserves end Dec.	13.0
Invisible outflows	-7.3	Foreign debt	40.6
Net transfers	7.7	as % of GDP	104.8
Current account balance	2.3	Debt service	4.7
as % of GDP	6.3	as % of export earnings	15.2

Principal exports[b]	$m fob	Principal imports[b]	$m cif
Petroleum & products	1,803	Transport equipment &	
Cotton yarn & textiles	450	machines	2,547
Engineering products	364	Livestock, food & drink	1,877
Agricultural goods	161	Fats, oils & minerals	1,267
Raw cotton	37	Chemicals, rubber & leather	1,107
		Wood, paper & textiles	1,100
Total	3,417	Total	10,732

Main export destinations	% of total	Main origins of imports	% of total
Italy	17.8	United States	21.4
United States	12.9	Germany	10.0
India	8.4	Italy	9.3
France	5.7	France	8.0
United Kingdom	5.5	Japan	5.8

Government

System Republic. Legislative unicameral People's Assembly elected for a 5-year term. Executive branch composed of president, prime minister and Cabinet.

Main political parties National Democratic Party (NDP), Socialist Labour Party, Liberal Socialist Party, Progressive Unionist Party, New Wafd Party, Nasserite Arab Democratic Party

Climate and topography

Hot, dry summers with moderate winters. Desert plateau interrupted by Nile Valley and Delta.

People and society

Population m	55.8	% under 15	37.9
Pop. per sq km	56	% over 65	4.2
% urban	44	No. men per 100 women	103
% av. ann. growth 1987–92	2.4	Human Development Index	55.1
No. households m	9.7		

Life expectancy		Education	
Men	65 yrs	Spending as % of GDP	6.7
Women	67 yrs	Mean years of schooling	3
Crude birth rate	26	Adult literacy %	50
Crude death rate	7	Primary school enrolment %	101
Infant mortality rate	57	Secondary school enrolment %	80
Under-5 mortality rate	93	Tertiary education enrolment %	19

Workforce	% of total	Consumer goods ownership	
Services	37	Telephone mainlines per 1,000	33
Industry	21	Televisions per 100	10.9
Agriculture	42		
% of total population	31		

Ethnic groups	% of total	Religious groups	% of total
Eastern Hamitic	90	Sunni Muslim	94
Greek, Italian or Syro-Lebanese	10	Coptic Christian & other	6

Tourism		Health	
Tourist receipts $m	2,730	Pop. per doctor	1,320
		Low birthweight babies % of total	10
		Daily calories % of total requirement	133
		% pop. with access to safe water	90

a 1988.
b Fiscal year ending June 30th.

IRAN

Total area	1,648,000 sq km	Population	61.4m
GDP	$47bn	GDP per head	$765
Capital	Tehran	Other cities	Mashhad, Esfahan, Tabriz

Having passed through a period of acute instability – a puritanical revolution followed by a disastrous war – Iran is simmering with discontent and facing an economic crisis. Its religious rulers have become increasingly enmeshed in questions such as rescheduling debts to western governments that they cannot service, holding down inflation and creating more jobs. Their radicalism, and their support for Islamic fundamentalism abroad, may diminish.

History: ancient empires

Iran's history stretches back to 533BC when Cyrus founded the first Persian empire. The Persians captured Egypt in 525BC and were ousted from power by Alexander in 330BC. He burnt the Persians' capital, Persepolis. The Zoroastrian religion predominated until Muslim Arabs invaded and took over in 637AD. The Persian language became established by the 10th century. By the 16th century the Persians were trying to establish a separate power centre, distinct from the Ottoman Turks. Ismail Safavi (1502–24) imposed Shia Islam on a predominantly Sunni population. In the 18th and 19th centuries Persia (as it then was) became strategically important. Britain, anxious to protect the approaches to India, wanted Persia to be either under British influence or firmly independent. Russia was attracted to the northern part. And the British worried about French and German interest. Monopolies were granted to foreigners to pay for the extravagances of the court, stirring up a nationalist reaction; the main bank had British capital. In 1907 Britain and Russia split the country into three spheres of influence: the north for Russia, the south for Britain and the centre for both. This went down badly with the Persians, who had no wish to see these encroachments.

The nation state

Iran's first modern ruler was Reza Shah (1925–41). He took over a number of foreign concessions, struck better bargains for some of them, imposed national military service, began to build a cross-country railway and allowed women not to wear the veil. In 1941 Reza Shah did not comply with an allied demand to expel all but a minimum number of Germans from the country and was forced out of office. He was succeeded by his son, Muhammad, as shah. After the second world war British and American occupying troops withdrew from the south, but it was only in 1946 that Soviet forces withdrew from the north.

The oil crisis

In 1949, after a revision of the government's contract with the dominant Anglo-Iranian Oil Company was signed, pressure grew for the oil wells and installations to be nationalised. It was led by the mercurial Muhammad Mossadegh, who became prime minister in 1951 and was ousted, in a movement orchestrated by American and British agents, two years later. A new oil agreement was made with a new company in which American companies had a leading role. The shah, to the surprise of many, survived and became a dominant figure, appointing and dismissing prime ministers. Trying to be a moderniser like his father, he set up two somewhat artificial political parties, one pro-government and the other opposed. He signed a security agreement with the United States, which began to supply his government with large quantities of arms. The shah also distributed his huge estates to the peasants and arranged for other big landowners to do likewise. Oil revenues continued to pour in and the shah, full of confidence, had himself crowned in 1967 in a vulgar ceremony that went down badly with the population, as did his grandiose celebration in 1971 of the 2,500th anniversary of the Persian monarchy.

The fall of the shah

The shah committed the basic error of failing to present himself to the people as a devout Muslim. The shah preferred to appear as a moderniser, who believed in the liberation of women (up to a point) and as a leader who wanted Iran to adopt western styles. None of this found favour among the majority of the population, which was poorly educated and devout. When he preened himself on the "peacock throne" he did not win sympathy. By liberalising the regime he allowed his enemies room for manoeuvre. Those who went too far suffered beatings and torture at the hands of his secret police, Savak, and the victims did not forget. The oil-price explosion of 1972–73 did not win him any friends. Finally there was a man opposed to the shah who symbolised a return to a medieval, uncomplicated and uncorrupted Islamic past and a rejection of modernism: Ayatollah Ruhollah Khomeini. Opposition grew, the army hesitated, the Carter administration was indecisive, and the shah went into exile in 1979. Khomeini returned home from Paris and the Islamic Republic, a government of Muslim clerics, was founded.

The embassy hostages

Khomeini was consumed by a hatred of the United States, for its role as the armourer and defender of the shah. The United States was dubbed the "Great Satan". On November 4th 1979 a crowd of "students" broke into the American embassy in Tehran and seized 53 hostages. They demanded the return of the shah to face trial. There was little that a deeply embarrassed President Carter could do. He could not mount an invasion, and even if he had been able to it would have amounted to a death sentence for the hostages. So he plumped for a commando raid in the hope that a top-flight team could land near Tehran, drive to the embassy, overpower the guards, free the hostages and come home. This scheme collapsed with engine failure. A helicopter collided with an aircraft. Eight men died. It was the Carter administration's darkest moment. Eventually the Iranians released the hostages in January 1981, after long negotiations and possibly because they were scared of what President Carter's hardline successor, Ronald Reagan, might unleash on them when he took office.

The Islamic republic

Under a new constitution, approved in 1979, Iran was to be run by a spiritual leader (Ayatollah Khomeini), a president, a prime minister, an elected parliament and a committee of clerics who would check on new laws to make sure that they conformed with the teachings of Shia Islam. Strict rules were introduced. Alcohol and fornication were banned. Women had to follow a strict dress code. However, the immense influence of Khomeini could not prevent bitter rivalries erupting among Iran's new rulers. Bombs exploded in Tehran. President Abolhassan Bani-Sadr was ousted and fled to Paris.

The regime seemed to be tottering, but was united by an invasion in 1980 by Iraq. The Iraqi president, Saddam Hussein, hoped that he could eliminate what he saw as a Shia-Iranian threat to his Sunni-dominated government and that he might even gain power over Iran. He was wrong. As many as 1m people may have lost their lives in the Iran-Iraq war, which ended with a ceasefire in 1988. Many thousands of young soldiers willingly sought martyrdom on the burning sands of the Iran-Iraq border. In the end the two sides reverted to their old borders. Iraq continued to help the anti-Khomeini exile movement, the Mujahideen e-Khalq (National Council of Resistance), which has its own National Liberation Army comprising 4,500 fighters.

Khomeini's successors

Ayatollah Khomeini's death in 1989, at the age of 87, left a political and religious vacuum. Before his death, he injected some poison into Anglo-Iranian relations by declaring a *fatwa* against a British citizen, Salman Rushdie, whose book, *The Satanic Verses*, was deemed to be blasphemous. Khomeini urged Muslims the world over to kill Mr Rushdie. They did not do so. Khomeini's job as Iran's spiritual leader went to President Ali Khamenei, though with a lower rank than Khomeini. He was also made an ayatollah (much to the dismay of the elderly grand ayatollahs who viewed him as a jumped-up politician). Khamenei's old post as president went to the pragmatic prime minister, Ali Akbar Hashemi Rafsanjani, who easily won the presidential election of 1989. He quickly formed a government and consolidated his position. Mr Rafsanjani wanted to see the Islamic Republic stimulate the lagging economy. He knew the population was tired of war and the demands of the revolution and wanted a better life. The president put the emphasis on economic reconstruction through a five-year development plan. He was re-elected in 1993.

Politics: conservatives versus pragmatists

Although Ayatollah Khomeini expressed his disapproval of political parties, they were nonetheless allowed to exist. The Islamic Republican Party was established by, among others, Rafsanjani and Khamenei, but it was split between radicals who wanted to impose state economic controls at home and spread revolutionary Islam abroad, and moderates who favoured free-market reforms and a less adventurous foreign policy. It was disbanded. The opposition Freedom Movement, founded by Mehdi Bazargan, the first prime minister under Khomeini and a genuine Muslim democrat, was barely tolerated. The exiled and respected leader of the National Front, Shahpour Bakhtiar, was assassinated in Paris in 1991; Iranian government officials were alleged to have been involved. Iranian agents were also suspected of killing exiled leaders of the Kurdish Democratic Party in Europe.

The toughest opponent of Mr Rafsanjani is Hojatoleslam Ali Akbar Mohtashemi, who is said to have close contacts with the Shia extremist group Hizbullah in Lebanon. Among Iran's influential political groups are the Tehran Militant Clergy Society, which is led by a pragmatist and has the backing of many business people, and the Association of Combatant Clergymen, which is led by a radical former parliamentary speaker.

The struggle continues

In 1994 continuing power struggles within the leadership added to President Rafsanjani's troubles over the shaky economy, forcing his brother's resignation from the influential post of head of state radio and television. An apparent attempt to kill the president raised questions about how extensive the clandestine opposition might be. Occasionally riots erupt in an interior town. Various explanations are offered. The most likely one is that the weak economy, failing to create urgently needed new jobs, has turned into a breeding ground for troublemakers of all varieties. Like the shah, Iran's rulers run a tough political police. The UN Commission on Human Rights said in 1994 that Iran had 19,000 political prisoners in a jail population of about 100,000. An author who had circulated open letters denouncing censorship and lack of freedom was arrested in 1994 on charges of drug-trafficking, homosexuality and espionage.

Foreign policy: mixed signals

The only explanation for Iran's confused foreign policy is that too many people are meddling. On one hand Iran poses as a serious country, signing or talking about oil and gas pipeline deals with the newly independent ex-Soviet republics and rescheduling its foreign debts. On the other hand Iran has been accused of being linked to terrorist attacks on anti-government exiles in France and Switzerland. A bomb blast in Buenos Aires in 1994 was at first blamed on Iran but subsequently Argentine officials said they had no evidence for their allegation. Iran's seizure of some contested Gulf islands, Abu Musa and the Greater and Lesser Tumbs, in 1972 and its claim to sovereignty over them in 1992 went down badly in the United Arab Emirates, which also claims them. Iran's relations with Saudi Arabia, across the Gulf, have always been strained but in the mid-1990s seemed to be on the mend.

Iran's armed forces remain worryingly large with some 528,000 servicemen. Iran has taken delivery of the latest Russian Mig-29s and Su-24s as well as Chinese F-7s and bought three Russian Kilo-class submarines.

Society: population worries

Before the 1979 revolution the shah had launched a programme that cut population growth from 3.1% a year in 1966 to 2.7% a year in 1976. Ayatollah Khomeini condemned this as a western plot. He halved the legal marriage

age for women from 18 to nine, banned contraceptives and dissolved the family-planning network. In the 1980s the population unsurprisingly surged by 3.9% a year. More than half of Iran's present population was born after the revolution. For the period 1987–92, population growth was a less calamitous 2.4%. It subsequently slipped to 2.7%. But in Tehran province the population rose from 7m in 1986 to 10.4m in 1991. Additional jobs will have to be created when these children join the workforce: the time-bomb is ticking.

The economy: in poor shape

Official figures put inflation in 1993–94 at 23%; foreign experts reckon it was in the 30–70% range depending on the sector. About 14% of the workforce was unemployed, which was no change from the 1986 figure despite vigorous efforts to create jobs. The outlook was fairly bleak. Iran found it could not service its foreign debt of some $20 billion and had to reschedule its debt arrangements with Germany, Japan, Austria, Switzerland and Spain. More such bills will fall due and Iran will have to reschedule them.

The government's chances of getting medium-term credits from western governments are thin. This will inhibit ambitious economic expansion plans, especially for Iran's large oil and gas reserves. The increasingly assertive parliament approved Mr Rafsanjani's 1994 budget but with a blank in the place where the government's revenue should be projected. This is because exchange rate changes have thrown the estimates into doubt. The intention had been to balance the budget. That appeared to be impossible.

Rafsanjani's gloom

According to the rumour-mill in Tehran's bazaars, Mr Rafsanjani offered three times to resign in 1994 and was turned down, presumably by Ayatollah Khamenei. The president was under strong pressure to achieve economic growth. GDP estimates vary widely, but not much growth was expected in the late 1990s. Much depended on the world price of oil. If Iraq was allowed by the UN Security Council to resume oil exports, the price could plummet.

Total area	1,648,000 sq km	% agricultural area	8
Capital	Tehran	Highest point metres	Qollehh-ye
Other cities	Mashhad, Esfahan,		Damavand 5,604
	Tabriz, Shiraz	Main rivers	Atrak, Karun,
			Qezel Owzan

The economy

GDP $bn	47.0	GDP per head $	765
% av. ann. growth in		GDP per head in purchasing	
real GDP 1985–93	1.1	power parity $	...

Origins of GDP[a]	% of total	Components of GDP[a]	% of total
Agriculture	17.8	Private consumption	55.0
Industry	35.2	Public consumption	14.5
of which:		Investment	29.1
manufacturing	...	Exports	24.1
Services	47.0	Imports	-22.8

Production average annual change 1985–93, %

Agriculture	4.0	Manufacturing	8.5
Industry	6.8	Services	1.3

Inflation and exchange rates

Consumer price 1993 av. ann. incr.	20.3%	Rials per $ av. 1994	1,748.75
Av. ann. rate 1988–93	18.6%	Rials per SDR av. 1994	2,525.78

Balance of payments, reserves, aid and debt

			$bn
Visible exports fob	19.9	Capital balance	4.9
Visible imports fob	-23.3	Overall balance	-0.2
Trade balance	-3.4	Change in reserves	-0.2
Invisible inflows	0.9	Level of reserves end Dec.	5.2
Invisible outflows	-5.9	Foreign debt	20.5
Net transfers	2.0	as % of GDP	52.6
Current account balance	-6.5	Debt service	1.6
as % of GDP	-5.0	as % of export earnings	7.2

Principal exports[b]	$bn fob	Principal imports[b]	$bn cif
Fuels	14.2	Manufactures	17.8
Non-fuel primary products	1.2	Non-fuel primary products	3.8
Manufactures	0.6		
Total	16.0	Total	21.7

Main export destinations	% of total	Main origins of imports	% of total
Japan	14.8	Germany	17.5
France	8.8	Japan	10.3
Italy	8.4	Italy	9.1
Netherlands	7.2	UAE	7.0
South Korea	6.7	United Kingdom	5.3
Germany	4.9	France	5.1

Government
System Theocratic republic. Supreme authority rests with the Spiritual Leader (*wali faqih*). President, who is elected for 4-year term, is head of the executive branch. Unicameral Consultative Assembly (Majlis ash-Shoura) also elected for 4 years.
Main political parties No officially recognised political parties.

Climate and topography
Mostly arid or semi-arid; tropical along the Caspian coast. Rugged mountainous rim; high central basin with deserts, small plains along both coasts.

People and society
Population m	61.4	% under 15	45.9
Pop. per sq km	37	% over 65	3.8
% urban	58	No. men per 100 women	104
% av. ann. growth 1987–92	2.4	Human Development Index	67.2
No. households m	...		

Life expectancy		Education	
Men	69 yrs	Spending as % of GDP	4.1
Women	70 yrs	Mean years of schooling	3.9
Crude birth rate	33	Adult literacy %	56
Crude death rate	6	Primary school enrolment %	112
Infant mortality rate	65	Secondary school enrolment %	57
Under-5 mortality rate	88	Tertiary education enrolment %	12

Workforce	% of total	Consumer goods ownership	
Services	44	Telephone mainlines per 1,000	40
Industry	26	Televisions per 100	6.5
Agriculture	30		
% of total population	26		

Ethnic groups	% of total	Religious groups	% of total
Persian	51	Shia Muslim	95
Azerbaijani	25	Sunni Muslim	4
Kurd	9		

Tourism		Health	
Tourist receipts $m	60	Pop. per doctor	3,140
		Low birthweight babies % of total	9
		Daily calories % of total requirement	134
		% pop. with access to safe water	89

a 1992.
b 1991.

IRAQ

Total area	438,445 sq km	Population	19.8m
GDP	$18.0bn	GDP per head	$864
Capital	Baghdad	Other cities	Basrah, Kirkuk, Mosul

Endowed with a tenth of the world's proven oil reserves, Iraq should be a rich and successful country, generously aiding the less well-off. Instead, it became in the 1990s one of the world's few pariah countries, suffering from severe trade sanctions, its oil output paralysed, its foreign debt of over $85 billion unpayable and its people hungry and jobless. The blame fell on one man alone, President Saddam Hussein, a rash and brutal dictator who took his country into two wars, and lost both. He remained in power by killing or terrorising possible rivals and by promoting himself in one of the world's last remaining personality cults.

History: Nebuchadnezzar was there

Since the third millennium various civilisations have left their mark on what is now Iraq. There were the Sumerians (founders of urban civilisation and inventors of writing), the Akkadians, the Elamites, the Amorites, the Mitani, the Hittites and the Assyrians, who came from north of present-day Baghdad. The main town was Babylon. In the fertile land between the Tigris and Euphrates rivers, known by the Greeks as Mesopotamia, some of the seeds of western civilisation grew and spread. Some great names ruled the area: Nebuchadnezzar (604–538BC), Alexander the Great (334–327BC), Trajan (113–117AD), the Abbasid caliphate, which promoted commerce, industry, arts and science (750–1258), and a grandson of Genghis Khan (1258–1335), who devastated the area. After Islam swept through in 637AD, the region became a battleground for rival followers of the Prophet Muhammad. The Persians and Ottoman Turks subsequently fought over Iraq's "fertile crescent" but eventually, in 1535, the Turks prevailed. They stayed in Baghdad until unseated by the British during the first world war.

For the first time in its history Iraq was ruled with British administrative methods, which were much disliked by both Arab nationalists and loyal servants of the former Ottoman Empire. These two groups did not like it when, at the San Remo conference in 1920, Britain was given a mandate to rule Iraq. They liked it even less when Prince Feisal, a Hashemite from the distant Hejaz (in present-day Saudi Arabia), was made king of Iraq in 1921 by the British. A year later the unusual Neutral Zone was created with British help in an area disputed by Iraq and Abdulaziz Ibn Saud. The zone's 7,000 sq km was demilitarised and available to nomads. It now produces large quantities of oil which is shared by Iraq and Saudi Arabia.

The rise of modern Iraq

With the help of the British, a constitution was drawn up and a treaty of friendship was signed, giving Britain a special position in the country. The British gave up their mandate and Iraq joined the League of Nations in 1932. The Iraqis made a hash of democracy. A tribal revolt was smashed in 1936, when a general seized power and was soon assassinated. Before and during the second world war, Iraq took an ambivalent attitude to its close ally, Britain, and seemed open to advances from the Germans. So the British occupied Baghdad in 1941. They subsequently withdrew but maintained influence in the Iraqi capital. They did not stop Iraqi troops being sent in 1948 to join Arab forces trying to prevent Jews in Palestine from creating the state of Israel. But the British encouraged the signing, in 1955, of the anti-Soviet Baghdad Pact by Iraq, Turkey, Iran and Pakistan. This went down poorly with the nationalists, as did the abortive Anglo-French-Israeli operation to seize and keep control of the Suez Canal in 1956.

The king, Feisal II, and his prime minister, Nuri es-Said, were deemed to be in the pocket of the British. In 1958 both men were assassinated in a military coup. The new military ruler, Abdel Karim Kassem, withdrew Iraq from the Baghdad Pact in 1959. A Kurdish revolt landed Kassem in trouble and he was replaced in 1963 by Colonel Abdel Salim Aref. The new boss tried to adopt the line of the Baath Socialist Party, whose ideas came from a Christian Syrian intellectual, Michel Aflaq, in the 1940s. Aref set up a Revolutionary Command Council to run the country in association with the Baath Party.

They liked a fight

After Israel's success in the 1967 Middle East war, Iraq cut relations temporarily with America and Britain. A year later Aref's government was ousted in a bloodless coup in which his prime minister, Ahmad Hassan al-Bakr, took over. There was talk of plots; ex-ministers were murdered and jailed. Iraqi politics became a ruthless, bloody business. Foreign policy was just as hard: Iraq gave total support to the Palestinians and rebuffed peace moves. Relations with neighbouring Syria, which had a rival Baath Party, turned sour. Syria established close relations with Iran, and closed down a pipeline carrying Iraqi oil across its territory to the Mediterranean. The next coup attempt was in 1973, when the defence minister was killed. Relations with the Kurds, in the north of the country, turned to war in 1974 when the Iraqis offered the Kurdish leaders a deal that fell short of their demand for full membership of the Revolutionary Command Council. The Kurds were helped by neighbouring Iran. Iraq's emerging strongman, the vice-president, Saddam Hussein, was worried. In 1975 he and the shah of Iran agreed at a meeting in Algiers to end their dispute over who controlled the Shatt al-Arab waterway at the head of the Gulf. Iraq had claimed it all. Under the new agreement the frontier would run down the middle of the main navigation channel. In return the shah agreed to stop helping the Kurds, and kept his word. This agreement was, however, only a temporary Iraqi concession: Saddam Hussein was working on other ideas. In 1979 he ousted al-Bakr and took over as president. Several senior leaders were murdered.

The Iran-Iraq war

Saddam Hussein was increasingly fearful that Iraq's Shia Muslims, living mainly in the south, would be infected by the Shia radicalism of Iran's Ayatollah Khomeini. This mattered because the Shia are Iraq's largest religious group; most people in the south, at Basra and two holy cities, Najaf and Karbala, are Shia. At the same time, Saddam Hussein was annoyed that Iran would not withdraw from a border town as agreed in the 1975 Algiers pact. Probably for both reasons, the Iraqi dictator launched his armed forces at Iran on a 480km (300-mile) front in 1980. They ran into stiff resistance and he decided to withdraw them in 1982. In the same year, however, Iran launched attacks on Iraq and followed them up on a wider front in 1982. Both sides attacked each other's oil installations at the head of the Gulf and sporadically attacked shipping.

Out of fear of Iran's medieval Ayatollah, most governments sided with Iraq's brutal strongman. Saudi Arabia and Kuwait are said to have contributed $30 billion to Iraq. America is said to have given Iraq hundreds of satellite photographs of Iranian troop movements. Iraq bought arms wherever it could find them: from its ever-closer friend Russia, from France, Brazil and China. Iraqi aircraft attacked two dozen Iranian towns. Iran retaliated with missiles and artillery and land assaults by tens of thousands of young infantrymen ready to become "martyrs" and go straight to heaven. Losses on both sides were heavy; raw recruits were mown down by machinegun fire. Finally a ceasefire was agreed in August 1988 and two years later Saddam Hussein unexpectedly agreed to Iran's terms. The two sides restored diplomatic relations. Saddam Hussein had other ambitions.

Next came Kuwait

In 1990 Iraq complained that Kuwait was not only pumping much more oil than the quota it had agreed with the Organisation of Petroleum Exporting Countries and thus depressing the world price, but it was also pumping oil from border land which belonged to Iraq. Worried by Iraq's menacing tone, Egypt's President Hosni Mubarak hurried to Baghdad and tried to mediate, to no avail. On August 2nd 1990 an overwhelming Iraqi force took over Kuwait and seemed about to invade north-east Saudi Arabia, where most of that country's oil reserves are located. President Bush rushed American forces to Saudi Arabia, at King Fahd's request and with the support of the UN Security Council, to fortify the border. He also assembled a "coalition" of some 30 countries opposed to the annexation of Kuwait, the leading members being Britain and France. The Arab world was split: a resolution of the Arab League condemning Iraq was easily approved but without the votes of Jordan, Yemen, the Palestine Liberation Organisation and Mauritania. Some Arabs did not feel sorry for the Kuwaitis, who were seen by critics to be rich and arrogant. Jordanians and Palestinians were excited by Saddam Hussein's propagandistic offer to pull out of Kuwait if Israel would pull out of the Gaza strip and the West Bank.

The "coalition" imposed a Security Council-backed blockade and comprehensive sanctions on Iraq. They had no immediate effect. The borders of Iraq's neighbours, Jordan, Turkey and Iran, proved to be porous. On November 29th the Council authorised UN members to use "all necessary means" to end the Iraqi occupation. They did. Operation Desert Storm started on January 16th 1991 with air and missile atttacks, followed up (when these did not have the desired result) with a land offensive on February 24th. The Iraqi soldiers fled. The allied forces liberated Kuwait and entered Iraq and were advancing on Basra when President Bush announced a ceasefire on February 28th.

The regime survived

A revolt by Shia Muslims in the south of Iraq and by Kurds in the north-east erupted. But Iraq's army had retreated from the allied force and had not been destroyed. Such was Saddam Hussein's grip on power, his personality cult and his willingness to eliminate any opponent that he not only kept power but also deployed the army in the south, where it put down the rebellion. In the north, the Kurds were better organised and received aid across the Turkish frontier. Western governments, led by Britain, established a "safe haven" for the Kurds and told Saddam Hussein to keep out of it. He obeyed, but mounted an economic blockade of the region. In the south the western powers created a "no-fly zone" below the 36th parallel, where they said Iraqi warplanes could not fly. Saddam Hussein's response was to press on with construction of a causeway and a canal that would divert waters entering the marshes of southern Iraq, and drain them. This made some 30,000 Shia rebels who had taken refuge there look elsewhere; many were detained by the army. Large numbers of refugees fled from the marshes to Iran.

Saddam Hussein's action appeared to spell the end of the community of "marsh Arabs" (*madan*), the indigenous inhabitants whose way of life can be traced back several thousand years to Sumerian civilisation. They support themselves by fishing, growing rice and making reed mats; many travel through the reeds, bulrushes and floating water plants of the marshes by canoe. There was no evidence to show that the diversion of waters was linked to the reclamation of land; the idea was to open up the area for the Iraqi army. A UN investigator complained of "indiscriminate bombardment" of the marshes.

At the end of the war Iraq was given an opportunity to become internationally acceptable and to provide food and medical care for its people. It could have agreed to sell some of its blockaded oil, under international control, and buy food and medicine with some of the proceeds, provided that the distribution was under international supervision. Saddam Hussein rejected these terms. The people of Iraq paid the price in hunger, sickness, suffering and death. Iraq could also resume selling oil on the world market, again under international control, if it could prove to UN inspectors, led by Rolf Ekeus, that it had destroyed its "weapons of mass destruction" and its ability to use them, and recognised the state of Kuwait and its newly demarcated borders. The oil revenue would be allocated three ways: to pay war reparations by instalments to Kuwait; to pay for the UN's expenses; and to put hard currency in Iraq's central bank. In mid-1994 Iraq claimed it should be allowed to resume pumping. Several governments, including France's and Russia's, were anxious for sanctions to be lifted as soon as possible if only to enable Iraq to resume paying its big outstanding debts and to enable them to resume stalled investment projects. But all agreed that Iraq had not met all the UN terms. In 1994

Saddam Hussein inexplicably amassed Iraqi troops on the Kuwaiti border again and withdrew them when American troops arrived in Kuwait.

Society: divided

Iraq is hard to keep together. But a fair distribution of the country's oil riches and of political power should do the trick. The alternatives are a brutal dictatorship by a minority (Sadddam Hussein's choice), a political shambles or civil war. Much has been done: before its two wars, Iraq had established a welfare state of considerable quality. The Kurds, who are not Arabs and who have close (if complicated) ties with fellow Kurds in Iran and Turkey, will always pose a difficult problem. But the evidence suggests that they will accept a deal which gives them the powers, more or less, of a German regional government and some seats in the federal cabinet. The Shia Muslims have always been second-class citizens compared with the more powerful Sunnis in the north. Yet they stayed loyal in the Iran-Iraq war; their anger overflowed only after the war over Kuwait. A deal can be struck. The Sunnis of Baghdad are not in charge either. They are subordinate to the Saddam Hussein clan from the northern town of Tikrit. In a shake-up in 1993 the dictator's half-brother became interior minister, his son-in-law became minister of minerals and energy, his first cousin stayed on as defence minister and his youngest son ran the elite special security agency. Saddam Hussein later appointed himself as prime minister.

The economy: ruined

Before Iraq's two wars, the economy was designed by the state to expand oil production and at the same time to diversify out of dependence on oil and to spend state revenues on creating good government and a welfare state. To a considerable degree Iraq was achieving these goals. Large investments were being made in the oil industry and others, such as electricity and water supply. The welfare state was acquiring a reputation for competence. The only benefit brought by the wars was a relaxation of tight socialist controls on most sectors of the economy (in a 1987 reform). Otherwise they brought nothing but a subsistence economy and misery. In the mid-1990s Iraq was suffering what was described as "pre-famine" conditions. Prices were soaring, the value of the dinar was falling and the country was suffering from a crime wave as people became desperate.

Total area	438,445 sq km	% agricultural area	13
Capital	Baghdad	Highest point metres	Rawanduz
Other cities	Basra, Kirkuk, Mosul		3,658
		Main rivers	Tigris, Euphrates

The economy

GDP $bn[a]	18.0	GDP per head $[a]	911
% av. ann. growth in		GDP per head in purchasing	
real GDP 1985–93	...	power parity $	...

Origins of GDP[b]	% of total	Components of GDP[c]	% of total
Agriculture	5.1	Private consumption	52.7
Industry	72.9	Public consumption	30.0
of which:		Investment	21.9
manufacturing	11.6	Exports	24.6
Services	22.0	Imports	-29.1

Production *average annual change 1985–93, %*

Agriculture	...	Manufacturing	...
Industry	...	Services	...

Inflation[a] and exchange rates

Consumer price 1993 av. ann. incr.	75%	Dinars per $ av. 1994	0.31
Av. ann. rate 1989–93	46.7%	Dinars per SDR av. 1994	0.45

Balance of payments[b], reserves, aid and debt $bn

Visible exports fob	9.5	Capital balance	...
Visible imports fob	5.1	Overall balance	...
Trade balance	4.4	Change in reserves	...
Invisible inflows	...	Level of reserves end Dec.	...
Invisible outflows	...	Foreign debt	82.9
Net transfers	...	as % of GDP	460.1
Current account balance	-0.9	Debt service	161
as % of GDP	...	as % of export earnings	32.2

Principal exports[b]	$m fob	Principal imports[a]	$m cif
Crude oil	14,500	Civilian	5,000
		Military	2,700
Total	14,600	Total	7,700

Main export destinations[ad]	% of total	Main origins of imports	% of total
United States	28.5	Germany	13.3
Brazil	9.9	United States	10.7
Turkey	9.8	Turkey	9.2
Japan	7.8	France	8.7
Netherlands	7.4	United Kingdom	8.4
Spain	4.6	Japan	4.5

Government
System Republic, based on provisional constitution of 1968. The president is elected by the Revolutionary Command Council, the highest state authority. Cabinet is chosen by the president. Unicameral National Assembly has some legislative power.
Main political parties Baath Socialist Party

Climate and topography
Mild to cool winters with dry, hot summers. Northernmost regions experience cold winters. Mostly broad plains with reedy marshes in south-east and mountains along borders with Iran and Turkey.

People and society

Population m	19.8	% under 15	43.7
Pop. per sq km	45	% over 65	3.0
% urban	73	No. men per 100 women	104
% av. ann. growth 1987–92	3.1	Human Development Index	61.4
No. households m	...		

Life expectancy		Education	
Men	62 yrs	Spending as % of GDP	...
Women	64 yrs	Mean years of schooling	5
Crude birth rate	36	Adult literacy %	62.5
Crude death rate	6	Primary school enrolment %	111
Infant mortality rate	84	Secondary school enrolment %	48
Under-5 mortality rate	...	Tertiary education enrolment %	13

Workforce	% of total	Consumer goods ownership	
Services	67	Telephone mainlines per 1,000	...
Industry	19	Televisions per 100	7.2
Agriculture	14		
% of total population	24		

Ethnic groups	% of total	Religious groups	% of total
Arab	80	Shia Muslim	65
Kurdish	15	Sunni Muslim	32
Turkoman or other	5		

Tourism		Health	
Tourist receipts $m	20	Pop. per doctor	...
		Low birthweight babies % of total	...
		Daily calories % of total requirement	133
		% pop. with access to safe water	91

a Estimate.
b 1989.
c 1985.
d 1988.
Note: Trade, balance of payments and debt data are estimates based on limited and inconsistent information.

ISRAEL

Total area	20,770 sq km	Population	5.3m
GDP	$72.7bn	GDP per head	$13,760
Capital	Jerusalem	Other cities	Tel Aviv-Jaffa, Haifa

In 1995 the peoples of the Near East had an opportunity to end a long, tortured and bloody era in their history and replace it with an era of guarded peace. Already Israel had given up administrative control of two parts of the Occupied Territories, the Gaza strip and Jericho, on the West Bank. In October 1994 it signed a peace treaty with Jordan. There were hopes that Israel's next peace agreements would be with Syria and Lebanon. But there was always the danger that a new bout of blood-letting would set back the peace process.

History: it started with Abraham

Israel can be understood only in the context of the history of the Jews. Abraham, the first of the patriarchs, is said to have been instructed by God in about 2000BC to take his people from Ur, centre of the Chaldean civilisation, to Canaan. Abraham led his people through Canaan to more fertile Egypt where, eventually, they were enslaved by the Pharaohs. In about 1200BC Moses led the flight of the Jews from Egypt and bequeathed them a set of laws which became known as the Torah. After wandering in the desert, the Jews under Joshua and David took power over Canaan. David's son, Solomon, built the temple in Jerusalem. The kingdom of the Jews split in two on Solomon's death. Israel fell to the Syrians in 722BC; Judea was absorbed later. Jerusalem was destroyed in 586BC by the Babylonians under Nebuchadnezzar. Many Jews were deported to Babylon but some stayed on. Thus ended the first Jewish commonwealth; it had lasted about 100 years.

The Jews returned

After King Cyrus of Persia conquered Babylon, he allowed the captive Jews to return to Israel. Some 42,000 did so in 538BC. They rebuilt the temple (520–515BC). There followed 200 years of relative tranquillity under Alexander the Great (starting in 332BC), when Judea was almost autonomous, and under the Syria-based Seleucid empire. But King Antiochus IV plundered the temple, turned it over to the worship of Zeus and banned the observance of the Jewish religion. Under Judah Maccabee, the Jews defeated the Seleucids, retook Jerusalem and restored the temple (164BC). Judean independence was recognised in 142BC. A monarchy was established; Jewish power spread. But the Romans took over, allowing Jewish rulers considerable autonomy. It was during this period that Christians believe that Jesus was born in Bethlehem, proclaimed himself as the Messiah and was crucified in Jerusalem at the wish of Jewish religious leaders and with the permission of the Roman governor. Many Jews regarded Jesus as a leader of the Essene cult; Christians took him to be the son of God.

Eventually the Jews rebelled against Roman dominance. Nero sent his greatest general, Vespasian, to put down the revolt and, in 70AD, Roman forces killed thousands of Jews and destroyed the temple. At Masada, a rocky fortress in the desert, one group of Jewish fighters held out until the last moment in 73AD and then, preferring death to captivity, took their own lives. Many Jews were subsequently deported. The second commonwealth was over. Most Jews were barred from entering Jerusalem. Some managed to stay on, producing their version of the Talmud, including Jewish history, learning and traditions. But the Jews were dispersed; the *diaspora* began.

The Jews kept their belief in the Promised Land, their culture and their traditions and dreamed one day of reoccupying Jerusalem. They lived in small, often tightly knit communities, sometimes in ghettoes. They frequently prospered but also suffered from second-class citizenship, sporadic pogroms, mass expulsions and other acts of anti-Semitism which reached a climax during the second world war when, in an act of unparalleled evil, Hitler's Nazis killed 6m Jews in gas chambers.

The growth of Zionism

Persecution in the 19th century encouraged the growth of Zionism. In 1917 the British foreign secretary, Arthur Balfour, wrote a letter to Lord Rothschild, on behalf of the Zionist Federation. It said: "His Majesty's government view with favour the establishment in Palestine of a national home for the Jewish people and will use their best endeavours to facilitate the achievement of this object, it being clearly understood that nothing shall be done which may prejudice the existing civil and religious rights of existing non-Jewish communities in Palestine." Sceptics said the "Balfour Declaration" was self-contradictory. In 1923 Britain took over the League of Nations mandate to rule Palestine. Jewish immigration gathered momentum; Arab residents protested. The British tried and failed to stem the flow. The Jewish population grew from 83,000 in 1922 to 445,000 in 1939 and about 650,000 in 1948. Immigration was supervised by the Jewish

Agency. Militant Jews in the Stern gang and Irgun Zvai Leumi tried to make the mandate unworkable: the British headquarters at the King David hotel was blown up.

The Palestinians leave

The Irgun Zvai Leumi captured the village of Deir Yassin and killed its inhabitants, an act which spread terror among Palestinians and sparked off an exodus. A UN commission recommended in 1947 the establishment of a Jewish state and set out the boundaries, which included the Mediterranean coastline. The Arabs were outraged. They began fighting Jews, who began seizing land. In 1947 the British gave up the mandate and transferred Transjordan to the Arabs. The UN General Assembly approved a partition plan providing for Jewish and Palestinian independence by dividing Palestine into two states. The Palestinians and other Arabs rejected it. Nonetheless, David Ben Gurion, head of the Jewish Agency, declared the state of Israel in May 1948, on the eve of Britain's withdrawal. Ten minutes later the United States recognised Israel.

In the ensuing war of 1948–49 against the armies of Egypt, Syria and Transjordan, and a contingent from Saudi Arabia, Israel gained control of a larger area of Palestine than it had been allocated, including half of the designated international zone of Jerusalem. Jordan took over the other half, and the West Bank. A year after Israel's establishment, elections were held. The Jews were back in control of part of Jerusalem for the first time since 70AD. But by the time the mandate had expired 400,000 Palestinians had become refugees; after independence, another 400,000 are said to have fled. The hostility of the Arab world was total. The seeds of Palestinian terrorism were planted. In 1964 the Palestine Liberation Organisation (PLO) was founded.

Suez and the Six-day war

In 1956, after Egypt's President Nasser had nationalised the Suez Canal, Britain and France (the principal shareholders) conspired with Israel to try to restore control of the Suez Canal Company. Israel invaded Egypt and almost reached the Canal; Britain and France moved their forces into the Canal Zone to "keep the combatants apart". Faced with the fury of President Eisenhower, however, all three countries withdrew. The next rash action came in 1967 when President Nasser ordered the UN peace-keeping force to leave Egypt's border with Israel and closed the Strait of Tiran, blocking access to the Gulf of Aqaba and Israel's port of Eilat. This amounted to an act of war. The Israelis invaded the Sinai desert and virtually wiped out the air forces of Egypt, Syria and Jordan. They captured East Jerusalem and the West Bank from Jordan, the Sinai from Egypt and the Golan Heights from Syria. About 380,000 Palestinians fled from the West Bank to Jordan. Subsequently the UN Security Council approved Resolution 242 which called ambiguously for the "withdrawal of Israeli armed forces from territories occupied during the recent conflict" (without specifying whether this meant "all" territories) in return for peace, an end to frontier claims and recognition of the right of "every state" (translation: Israel) to "live in peace within secure and recognised boundaries".

The Yom Kippur war and Camp David

In 1973 Egypt's President Anwar Sadat launched an attack across the Suez Canal against Israel with the aim of making gains on the ground and then negotiating a peace settlement from a position of strength. Surprising the Israelis on Yom Kippur, the holiest day of the Jewish calendar, Egyptian forces advanced into northern Sinai. At the same time, Israeli forces crossed the canal further south and advanced into Egypt, surrounding the Third Army. A separation-of-forces agreement was negotiated with the help of the American secretary of state, Henry Kissinger. This was followed up by President Sadat in 1977 with a historic visit to Jerusalem, where he repeated long-standing Arab demands in a speech to parliament. Two years later President Jimmy Carter invited Sadat and the Israeli prime minister, Menachem Begin, to Camp David, the presidential retreat in Maryland. The two adversaries signed a peace treaty under which Israel handed the Sinai peninsula back to Egypt and diplomatic relations were established.

Israel invades Lebanon

Israeli anger over terrorist and military attacks by the PLO, which had set up a "state within a state" in Lebanon, boiled over in 1982. The prime minister, Menachem Begin and his defence minister, Ariel Sharon, wanted to defeat the PLO once and for all. Israel's attack was a limited incursion but met little resistance and the Israelis surrounded Muslim West Beirut. After a long siege the PLO fighters were obliged to leave. Under Israeli eyes, Christian militiamen subsequently entered two Palestinian refugee camps, Sabra and Chatila, and massacred their civilian inhabitants. An Israeli inquiry later found that the government was indirectly responsible, by not having supervised the militias properly and by failing to react to reports of militiamen entering the camps.

War and peace

In 1987 the Palestinians in Gaza and the West Bank launched their uprising (*intifada*), provoked by decades of ill-treatment by the Israeli military authorities, poverty, unemployment and bad living conditions. It was also a protest against the establishment of large numbers of Israeli settlements on land in the West Bank, Gaza strip and Golan Heights. The *intifada* amounted to strikes, demonstrations and stone-throwing by boys. Israel's response was tough: hundreds of Palestinians were killed. (At the same time, many Palestinians suspected of working with the Israelis were killed by Palestinian extremists.) Nonetheless, a framework for peace talks was created at the Madrid conference in 1991: committees were formed for bilateral deals between Israel and its neighbours. The PLO was indirectly represented by Palestinians in a joint Jordanian-Palestinian delegation.

In 1993, however, after secret meetings in Norway, Israel and the PLO stunned the world by recognising each other and agreeing on a Declaration of Principles paving the way to a two-stage solution to the dispute. In the first stage in 1994, the PLO took charge of the Gaza strip and the West Bank town of Jericho. Yasser Arafat became president of the Palestine Authority. The next stage was to be to hold elections and negotiate a "final settlement" of the status of the West Bank with an elected Palestinian administration. But by early 1995 Israel had declined to withdraw its troops from the West Bank, a Palestinian pre-condition for elections to be held. Nonetheless, the agreement in Norway paved the way for Israel and Jordan to sign a peace treaty in October 1994. Still on the agenda was peace with Syria and Lebanon. The PLO tried to show it was serious about security. After Hamas extremists kidnapped an Israeli soldier in 1994 it was police of the PLO-led Palestine Authority, and not the Israelis, who detained more than 100 suspected Hamas members.

Politics: bitter rivals

Political power in Israel has swung between the Labour Party and the Likud grouping. But because Israel applies proportional representation, small parties have emerged whose votes are crucial to the formation of coalitions. In Israel's early years the dominant figure was Labour's David Ben Gurion, prime minister from 1948 to 1954. He was succeeded by Moshe Sharett (1954–55) but bounced back to power in 1955 and kept it until 1963. The uncharismatic Levi Eshkol was in office from 1963 to 1969, when the tough but much-loved Golda Meir took over. Yitzhak Rabin, former chief of staff and ambassador to Washington, came next (1974–77). Then a sea-change occurred: for the first time, Labour fell from power and Likud formed a government under Menachem Begin (1977–83). He wanted Israel to keep the West Bank forever and vigorously promoted settlements there. He was followed by Likud's equally hard-line Yitzhak Shamir, who served from 1983 to 1984 and, after two years of Labour's Shimon Peres, from 1986 to 1992. In that year Mr Rabin, who was seen as tougher on the Palestinians than Mr Peres, returned to office with Mr Peres as his foreign minister. Mr Rabin and Mr Peres, often bitter rivals, worked together successfully. They were jointly awarded the Nobel peace prize with Yasser Arafat in 1994.

Society: visions of Zion

Socialist Zionism represented the dominant political force in the Jewish community by the 1920s. It was linked to trade unionism. Its political successor is the Labour Party. Nationalist Zionism, reflecting the ideas of Ze'ev Jabotinsky, was espoused by Begin and Shamir. Religious Zionism, represented by the National Religious Party, sees Israel as the fulfilment of God's will. The Israeli Arabs were at one time linked to the Israeli Communist Party, but are now on their own. They support co-existence between Arabs and Jews in Israel, and the establishment of a Palestinian state.

Economy: free but controlled

Israel's economy is mixed. There is a strong co-operative sector including the *kibbutzim*, a unique form of collective farm. The economy has always been burdened by the need for heavy military expenditure. This has, however, been offset by aid from Jews in the *diaspora*, who buy government bonds, and by American aid of $3 billion a year. After rapid expansion in the first 25 years, with GDP growing at 9–10% a year, growth slumped after the 1973 war for a decade. In the first half of the 1980s Israel was heading for hyper-inflation. In 1985 an emergency programme brought the rate down from 15–20% a month to 15–20% a year. By 1990 the economy had recovered and investment was increasing. However, Israel has virtually no oil or natural gas and relies on imported fuel, and in 1993 the trade deficit was $5.6 billion, the current account deficit £1.4 billion, and foreign debt reached $26.5 billion, equivalent to more than 40% of GDP.

Total area	20,770 sq km	% agricultural area	22
Capital	Jerusalem	Highest point metres	Har Meron
Other cities	Tel Aviv-Jaffa, Haifa		1,208
		Main rivers	Jordan, Alexander, Hadera

The economy

GDP $bn	72.7	GDP per head $	13,760
% av. ann. growth in		GDP per head in purchasing	
real GDP 1985–93	4.6	power parity $	14,890

Origins of GDP	% of total	Components of GDP	% of total
Agriculture	2.4	Private consumption	63.1
Industry	30.3	Public consumption	28.8
of which:		Investment	23.8
manufacturing	...	Exports	33.6
Services	67.3	Imports	-49.3

Production *average annual change 1985–93, %*

Agriculture	...	Manufacturing	...
Industry	...	Services	...

Inflation and exchange rates

Consumer price 1993 av. ann. incr.	11%	New shekels per $ av. 1994	3.02
Av. ann. rate 1988–93	15.8%	New shekels per SDR av. 1994	4.35

Balance of payments, reserves, aid and debt

			$bn
Visible exports fob	14.8	Capital balance	0.5
Visible imports fob	-20.4	Overall balance	1.5
Trade balance	-5.6	Change in reserves	1.4
Invisible inflows	7.3	Level of reserves end Dec.	6.4
Invisible outflows	-9.9	Foreign debt	26.5
Net transfers	6.7	as % of GDP	40.7
Current account balance	-1.4	Debt service	3.2
as % of GDP	-1.9	as % of export earnings	14.4

Principal exports	$m fob	Principal imports	$m cif
Metal, machinery &		Investment goods	3,577
electronics	5,080	Diamonds	3,352
Diamonds	2,990	Consumer non-durables	2,528
Chemical goods	1,871	Fuel	1,742
Textiles, clothing & leather	932	Consumer durables	1,268
Agricultural goods	558		
Total	14,083	Total	20,245

Main export destinations	% of total	Main origins of imports	% of total
United States	30.9	United States	17.7
United Kingdom	5.5	Belgium/Luxembourg	12.2
Belgium/Luxembourg	5.4	Germany	10.4
Germany	5.3	United Kingdom	8.6

Government

System Republic. No formal constitution. Unicameral parliament (Knesset) elected for 4 years. Executive branch composed of president (elected for a 5-year term), prime minister and Cabinet.

Main political parties Labour Party, Likud, Meretz, Tzomet, Shas, National Religious Party, United Torah Jewry, Hadash, Moledet, Arab Democratic Party

Climate and topography

Temperate, hot and dry in desert areas. Negev desert in south, low coastal plain, central mountains, Jordan Rift Valley.

People and society

Population m	5.3	% under 15	28.8
Pop. per sq km	255	% over 65	9.7
% urban	92	No. men per 100 women	98
% av. ann. growth 1987–92	3.2	Human Development Index	90
No. households m	1.1		

Life expectancy		Education	
Men	75 yrs	Spending as % of GDP	6.0
Women	79 yrs	Mean years of schooling	10.2
Crude birth rate	21	Adult literacy %	95
Crude death rate	6	Primary school enrolment %	95
Infant mortality rate	9	Secondary school enrolment %	85
Under-5 mortality rate	13	Tertiary education enrolment %	34

Workforce	% of total	Consumer goods ownership	
Services	74	Telephone mainlines per 1,000	350
Industry	22	Televisions per 100	26
Agriculture	4		
% of total population	39		

Ethnic groups	% of total	Religious groups	% of total
Jewish	83	Jewish	82
Non-Jewish	17	Muslim	14

Tourism		Health	
Tourist receipts $m	1,876	Pop. per doctor	410
		Low birthweight babies	
		% of total	7
		Daily calories % of total	
		requirement	…
		% pop. with access to safe water	100

JORDAN

Total area	91,880 sq km	Population	4.3m
GDP	$4.9bn	GDP per head	$1,190
Capital	Amman	Other cities	Irbid, Zarqa

Jordan's survival as a modestly prosperous country with a fair amount of democracy in a volatile part of the world is due principally to one man: King Hussein. He has led his small and weak country with considerable skill through wars and crises, and survived several attempted assassinations. He has made peace with Israel.

History: the oldest town?

Jericho, on the west bank of the Jordan river, has a record of settlement starting in 9000BC. It may be the world's oldest town. The region fell under the Assyrians, the Baylonians, the Persians, the Seleucids and the Romans and subsequently the Muslim Arabs in the 7th century AD. It was the turn of the Crusaders in 1099, the Ottoman empire in the 16th century and the British during the first world war, when the Turks supported the Germans. The British sought Arab aid and, in an exchange of letters in 1916 between Sir Henry McMahon and Sherif Hussein of the Hejaz (now part of Saudi Arabia including Mecca and Medina), agreed to some mutual help. In return for Hussein's army attacking the Turks, Britain would send arms and support independence for the Arab people after the war was over. The British did not keep their word. Under the secret Sykes-Picot treaty of 1916, Britain and France distributed areas of influence in the Middle East to themselves, Palestine went to Britain. A year later, the British foreign secretary, Arthur Balfour, pledged British support for a home for world Jewry in Palestine. The Arabs felt betrayed.

Lawrence was there

In 1917 an Arab army took Aqaba, at the head of the Gulf of Aqaba, from the Turks. Led by the Hashemite Prince Faisal, son of Sherif Hussein, the army went on to capture Amman and occupy Damascus. With it was a British officer, T.E. Lawrence (later glamourised as Lawrence of Arabia). With British backing, Faisal was in 1921 declared to be king of Iraq (far from the Hejaz). His brother, Abdullah, became king of Transjordan in 1923. Britain recognised Transjordan to be independent in the same year. It was excluded from the scope of Balfour's pledge. Britain was given a mandate to rule Palestine, which was not part of Abdullah's territory, by the League of Nations in 1922. The house of Hashem suffered a grave reverse in 1924 when Sherif Hussein, after making a series of tactical errors, abdicated in favour of his third son, Ali. Both men went into exile as the advancing forces of Abdulaziz Ibn Saud, the future king of Saudi Arabia, absorbed the Hejaz into his realm. Britain granted Transjordan a greater degree of independence in 1928, but the British resident was always there, keeping an eye on things, and British generals trained the army to a high degree of military competence.

Jordan takes the West Bank...
After the second world war Transjordan applied for membership of the United Nations but questions were asked about its treaty tying it to Britain, and the request was vetoed by the Soviet Union. In 1945, however, Jordan helped to form the Arab League. Three years later the British, under attack from Jewish guerrillas and denounced by all sides for errors of omission or commission, handed their mandate over Palestine to the United Nations and withdrew their forces. The State of Israel was proclaimed, and the region was transformed. Arab armies entered Palestine and seized large parts of it. King Abdullah, whose forces had occupied much land on the West Bank of the Jordan, seemed ready to accept a ceasefire line. To underline his position, he changed his title to king of Jordan (Transjordan implying only the East Bank). He annexed the West Bank in 1950. In an east Jerusalem mosque in 1951, however, Abdullah was assassinated before the eyes of his grandson, Hussein. A year later the king's son and successor, Talal, who was mentally unbalanced, abdicated and Hussein became king at the age of 17.

...and loses it
The early years of Hussein's long reign were marked by sporadic instability stirred up by radical governments – Egypt, Syria and Iraq – and by the Palestinians of the West Bank, who did not relish being governed by a family from the poorly developed Hejaz. The loudest voices were those of pan-Arab, republican nationalists. The king had at times to depend on the army, which included many men of Bedouin origin. To show the Arab world his independence from the British, he abruptly dismissed his army commander, Lieut-General Sir John Glubb ("Glubb Pasha") in 1955. When Egypt's President Nasser provoked the calamitous 1967 war with Israel, Jordan was drawn in as well. It lost the West Bank. Thousands of Palestinian refugees poured

across the Jordan to the East Bank and the Palestine Liberation Organisation (PLO), led by Yasser Arafat, created a "state
within a state" there. PLO terror attacks, including the hijacking of three airliners and their destruction at Dawson's Field
in Jordan in 1970, caused serious embarrassment and the
PLO became a threat to the king's survival. In the same year
he launched a campaign against the PLO and drove most of
them, Yasser Arafat included, out of the country.

There followed a period of relative stability until 1973,
when Egypt's President Sadat launched an attack on the
Israeli-occupied Sinai desert without consulting Hussein.
Badly burnt by letting Jordan be drawn into Nasser's war
with Israel, the king stayed out this time. He symbolically
sent some troops to join Syria's reserves but that was all. A
year later he reluctantly accepted a decision by an Arab
summit at Rabat that the PLO was the sole legitimate representative of the Palestinian people. The Palestinians'
intifada (struggle), which started in 1987, had shown that
they looked to Mr Arafat rather than King Hussein for leadership. The king formally cut his government's links with
the West Bank, where Jordan had been continuing to pay
the salaries of local officials, in 1988, but did not abandon
Hashemite claims to the Israeli-occupied territory.

Politics: a pragmatic monarch

King Hussein's policies concerning internal security,
democracy and relations with Israel and the rest of the Arab
world were flexible. The 1952 constitution provided for a
free press and political parties but when the parties tried to
limit the king's powers in 1958, he banned them. During the
war with Israel in 1967, martial law was introduced. The
press was neutered. The government was said to be corrupt. Jordanians objected to authoritarianism. The government's adoption of austerity as the price for a loan from the
International Monetary Fund, when GDP slumped by 13.5%
in 1989, was the spark. Riots erupted outside Amman. Flexible as ever, the king fired his prime minister and called a
parliamentary election for the same year – the first since
1957. The election was free although political parties were
not allowed to take part. Twenty-one deputies came from
the (Islamist) Muslim Brotherhood and in all 34 deputies
were linked to Islamist groupings. Some became ministers
and learned at first hand the difficulties of governing with
limited resources. Another parliamentary election, including
parties, was held in 1993 and the Islamists lost ground. The
leading group was the Progressive Democratic Coalition (of

liberals and leftists) with 22 seats, followed by the National Action Front (led by a Jordanian nationalist), with 18 seats and, in third place, the Islamic Action Front, an Islamist umbrella group including the Muslim Brotherhood, with 16 seats. For the first time a woman, Taujan Faisal, won a seat.

Popularity has a price

The king is a constitutional monarch with a difference: he is also the ultimate arbiter. It is he who decides, in consultation with his brother, Crown Prince Hassan, and his close aides, on foreign and economic strategy. An all-embracing 1992 law requires the media to refrain from publishing news "harmful to the king or the royal family" or "anything contradicting the principles of freedom, national responsibility, human rights, respect for the truth and the values of the Arab and Islamic nation". Some prosecutions have been made, according to Amnesty International, and the security police are not gentle with people suspected of being subversive extremists. However, the king is no dictator; his political antennae are finely tuned and he rarely slips up. By holding elections and opening up Jordanian politics, he has gained stature and become more popular. When Iraq occupied Kuwait and offered to withdraw if Israel would withdraw from the West Bank and Gaza strip, King Hussein appeared to side with Saddam Hussein. Jordanians cheered him. (In 1994 the king was snubbed by King Fahd when he visited Saudi Arabia on a pilgrimage.)

Foreign policy: Israel and the Palestinians

King Hussein's attitude to Israel was for many years non-confrontational. He held sporadic but productive clandestine meetings with Israeli leaders. But at no time did he put his throne or himself in danger by taking the lead in signing a peace agreement with Israel. He left that to Egypt's Anwar Sadat, who broke the ice by going to Israel, addressing its parliament and agreeing on a peace treaty at Camp David (for which he was subsequently assassinated). It was only after Yasser Arafat agreed to a partial settlement with Israel in 1994, enabling the PLO to take over the Gaza strip and Jericho, that Hussein went ahead. He met the Israeli prime minister, Yitzhak Rabin, and President Clinton in Washington and both he and the Israeli leader addressed the American Congress. This went a long way to erasing American memories of the king's ambivalent attitude towards Iraq's occupation of Kuwait. The king signed a declaration ending the 46-year state of war with Israel and entered substantive negotiations over the few impediments to signing a peace treaty, among them the vexed question of water rights. The frontier was opened for tourists between Israel's Eilat and Jordan's adjacent Aqaba and at a bridge across the Jordan river. By moving faster than Syria in seeking a deal with Israel, however, the king risked annoying President Assad.

Perhaps Jordan's key role was yet to be played. In 1995 the future of the West Bank and Gaza strip was unclear. They could form a new Palestinian state under the leadership of the PLO. This would, however, worry many Israelis who are deeply suspicious of Mr Arafat. Much more acceptable would be some sort of loose confederation of Jordan and Palestine, on the assumption that King Hussein's "moderate" government would play a strong role in it. At the Middle East peace talks in Madrid in 1991, there was a joint Jordanian-Palestinian negotiating team. However, the pattern quickly emerged of the PLO negotiating separately with Israel, sometimes without consultation. On the Jericho-and-Gaza negotiation, Jordan was left out in the cold. This caused much irritation in Amman. For his part the king aggravated Mr Arafat by signing an agreement with Israel reaffirming his long-standing custodianship of the Muslim holy places in Jerusalem. The Jordanian dinar and the Israeli shekel remain as the two official currencies of the West Bank and Gaza strip; the PLO had no currency. Relations between the king and the PLO will remain bumpy.

Society: a question of percentages

It is not entirely clear who is a Jordanian, and how many Jordanians there are. True-blue Jordanians are those who were permanently resident in the country before the 1948 war led King Abdullah to absorb the West Bank, with its overwhelmingly Palestinian population. The Transjordanians included Bedouin tribesmen, ultra-loyal to the Hashemite dynasty. The 1948 war brought a vast influx of refugees who had been ousted from their homes by the Israelis. Thereafter the Palestinian population of Jordan grew and grew. There was an influx of roughly 200,000 Palestinians who had been working in Kuwait and were ousted, after the Iraqi occupation ended, because the PLO had supported Iraq.

How many Palestinians live in Jordan? Percentages vary wildly. By one reckoning Palestinians who came to Jordan since 1948 acccount for 37% of the population of about 4.3m; by another they account for 70%. The latter estimate suggests that the Palestinians are taking over; indeed one of

Jordan's prime ministers, Taher Masri, was a Palestinian. But the Palestinian residents of Jordan do not push their luck. They know very well that they are living in a stable, free and capitalist country and that this depends to a considerable extent on the king and his government.

The economy: fragile but open

The structural adjustment package agreed with the IMF in 1989 was designed to bring the budget deficit down from 18% of GDP to 5%. Spending would be cut and taxes would be increased. Consumption would be reduced sharply and inflation would go down from 10% to 4.5%. (By the fourth quarter of 1993 it was down to 5.7% on an annual basis and the IMF said it was pleased with Jordan's overall performance.) But the medicine was bitter and riots erupted. Nonetheless, the king, government and parliament persisted. Implementation was delayed by the Gulf war, renegotiation of the IMF agreement and the slowness of parliament in approving a sales tax. In 1994 parliament reduced the tax from 10% to 7% and ruled that a second-stage tax would be applied after five years had elapsed, rather than the original three. Since an election was due to be held in less than five years, this measure ensured that the deputies would not be blamed for the tax by the voters.

In any event government revenues seemed likely to be boosted by the steady growth of GDP: from -13.5% in 1989 to 11.2% in 1992 (caused by the arrival, with their savings, of Palestinians expelled by Kuwait) and 5.8% in 1993. Peace with Israel seemed certain to boost business confidence. As a thank-you for his appearance in Washington with President Clinton and the Israeli prime minister, the president asked Congress to forgive part of Jordan's debt to the United States. At a meeting organised by the World Bank, donor states pledged $200m to help Jordan to cover its expected current-account deficit in 1994 and 1995. Most worrying was the trade deficit, which reached $1.9 billion in 1993. Exports of chemicals, phosphates, potash and farm products are not enough. If ever a genuine regional peace settlement is achieved, however, the resulting boom should help to solve Jordan's difficulties.

Total area	91,880 sq km	% agricultural area	5
Capital	Amman	Highest point metres	Jabal Ram
Other cities	Irbid, Zarqa		1,754
		Main rivers	Jordan, Yarmuk

The economy

GDP $bn	4.9	GDP per head $	1,190
% av. ann. growth in		GDP per head in purchasing	
real GDP 1985–93	0.5	power parity $	4,010

Origins of GDP	% of total	Components of GDP	% of total
Agriculture	8.0	Private consumption	89.6
Industry	26.2	Public consumption	23.7
of which:		Investment	30.1
manufacturing	14.7	Exports	38.0
Services	65.8	Imports	-81.4

Production average annual change 1985–93, %

Agriculture	...	Manufacturing	...
Industry	...	Services	...

Inflation and exchange rates

Consumer price 1993 av. ann. incr.	4.7%	Dinars per $ av. 1994	0.70
Av. ann. rate 1988–93	11.5%	Dinars per SDR av. 1994	1.01

Balance of payments, reserves, aid and debt

			$bn
Visible exports fob	1.2	Capital balance	-0.7
Visible imports fob	-3.1	Overall balance	-0.4
Trade balance	-1.9	Change in reserves	0.9
Invisible inflows	1.7	Level of reserves end Dec.	1.7
Invisible outflows	-1.6	Foreign debt	6.9
Net transfers	1.4	as % of GDP	142.9
Current account balance	-0.5	Debt service	1.7
as % of GDP	-9.2	as % of export earnings	14.6

Principal exports	$m fob	Principal imports	$m cif
Food & live animals	202	Machinery & transport	
Phosphates	141	equipment	785
Potash	124	Manufactured goods	731
Manufactured goods	117	Chemicals	359
		Crude oil	342
Total	998	Total	3,542

Main export destinations	% of total	Main origins of imports	% of total
Saudi Arabia	11.6	United States	12.7
Iraq	11.2	Iraq	12.5
India	9.5	Germany	8.3
Indonesia	5.4	Japan	5.0

Government
System Constitutional monarchy. Executive power vested in the king, who governs with the assistance of an appointed council of ministers. Bicameral National Assembly consists of appointed Senate and elected House of Representatives.
Main political parties The Progressive Democratic Coalition, National Action Front, Islamic Action Front

Climate and topography
Cool winters and hot, dry summers; rainy season in the west (November to April). Mostly desert plateau in east, highland area in the west. Great Rift Valley of Jordan River separates East and West Banks.

People and society

Population m	4.3	% under 15	48.1
Pop. per sq km	48	% over 65	2.6
% urban	69	No. men per 100 women	110
% av. ann. growth 1987–92	3.1	Human Development Index	62.8
No. households m	...		

Life expectancy		Education	
Men	68 yrs	Spending as % of GDP	5.9
Women	72 yrs	Mean years of schooling	5
Crude birth rate	38	Adult literacy %	82.1
Crude death rate	5	Primary school enrolment %	97
Infant mortality rate	28	Secondary school enrolment %	91
Under-5 mortality rate	41	Tertiary education enrolment %	25

Workforce	% of total	Consumer goods ownership	
Services	64	Telephone mainlines per 1,000	75
Industry	26	Televisions per 100	8.1
Agriculture	10		
% of total population	23		

Ethnic groups	% of total	Religious groups	% of total
Arab	98	Sunni Muslim	92
Circassian	1	Christian	8

Tourism		Health	
Tourist receipts $m	462	Pop. per doctor	770
		Low birthweight babies % of total	7
		Daily calories % of total requirement	111
		% pop. with access to safe water	99

KUWAIT

Total area	17,820 sq km	Population	1.9m
GDP	$34.1bn	GDP per head	$23,350
Capital	Kuwait City	Other cities	Hawalli, Al-Salimiya

Having survived, with help from some powerful friends, Iraq's occupation in 1990–91, oil-rich Kuwait has begun to transform itself. It has acquired a new parliament, of sorts. It has started to worry about budget deficits and to charge for some welfare-state services. It has been accused of human-rights abuses including a Kuwaiti version of ethnic cleansing. The Sabah family remains in charge.

History: who wanted it?

Kuwait was for centuries nothing more than a bit of hot, dry and inhospitable Arabian desert, not associated with the fertile plains of what is now Iraq, watered by the Tigris and the Euphrates. Nomads lived there. What is now Kuwait city was probably settled in the 17th century by tribes which moved there from the interior. It was a small settlement based on trading and pearl fishing. Fresh water came from the distant Shatt al-Arab. The Sabah family's long rule began in 1756 when the settlers appointed a sheikh to manage their affairs and deal with the Ottoman ruler in Basra, the regional administrative capital. The British East India Company traded there. The Sabahs maintained a quasi-autonomous relationship with the Turks, although they paid tribute to Ottoman suzerainty. But in 1899 they switched to Britain and signed an agreement under which, in return for British protection against marauding tribes and aggressive imperialists, the sheikh would take no foreign-policy decision without British consent.

Everything changed

British protection did not prevent Kuwait losing some 40% of its territory to Saudi Arabia in the 1920s. Iraq, after its independence from Britain in 1932, laid claim to part of Kuwait, but got nowhere. In 1961 Kuwait's impending independence from Britain was challenged by Iraq and British troops were sent in. They were replaced by an Arab League force. The following year Kuwait became a member of the United Nations and the Arab League. Iraq tried again to take over Kuwait in 1990 but its forces, led by President Saddam Hussein, were ejected by American-led forces in February 1991.

It was in 1934 that everything changed for Kuwait when Sheikh Ahmad granted a concession to two oil companies, Gulf of the United States and Anglo-Persian of Britain, which formed the Kuwait Oil Company. Drilling was showing promise when the second world war intervened. It was resumed after the war ended and the oil gushed. Soon, under the imaginative if also extravagant Sabahs, Kuwait became a welfare state with free education, health care and local telephone calls as well as subsidised housing. Huge investments were made at home and abroad.

Not quite democratic

In 1961 Kuwait elected a 20-member constituent assembly which drafted a constitution under which a 50-seat National Assembly was elected, for the first time, in 1963. Another election was held in 1971. The electorate was odd: only adult males who could trace their ancestry to 1920 could vote. The assembly comprised 50 elected members plus cabinet ministers appointed by the amir. Usually about half of the cabinet members came from the Sabah family, which controlled key ministries. The crown prince was prime minister. Political parties were not permitted. Nonetheless, 184 candidates stood for election. The assembly was no rubber stamp. It challenged the Sabahs' pervasive influence but was unable to supplant it. Another election was held in 1975. The amir dissolved the assembly in 1976, for five years, grumbling that it had delayed legislation. Under public pressure, the amir agreed to hold another election in 1981. This time only 90,000 "first-class citizens" could vote. Less than half of them registered. Some of those who were elected continued to challenge the Sabahs in one way or another. Tensions grew: there was an attempt on the life of the amir in 1985 and bombs were detonated in the capital and the main refinery for exported oil. In 1986, after the assembly embarrassed the Sabahs by forcing the resignation of the justice minister (a member of the ruling family), the amir dissolved it again.

The occupation

Kuwait's armed forces in the 1970s were small and insignificant, based on irregulars. War between Iran and Iraq scared the Kuwaitis into arming themselves more seriously. They bought anti-aircraft missiles from the Russians, surface missiles from the Egyptians and a new air-defence system from the Americans. The armed forces comprised about 20,000 men. They included 18 Mirage-1 fighters and 24 helicopters. In January 1990 Iraq's President Saddam Hussein started sending signals of what was to come. Kuwait was breaking an agreement on oil production with the Organisation of Petroleum Exporting Countries, he said. Kuwait's overproduction had depressed the world price and Iraq demanded compensation. Kuwait was pumping oil and had erected military posts on land Iraq claimed. Attempts at mediation got nowhere. To the surprise of western intelligence services, Iraq invaded Kuwait with a force of roughly 100,000 men on August 2nd. The Kuwaiti armed forces collapsed in the face of overwhelming Iraqi strength. The amir, his family and his ministers fled to Saudi Arabia. There were widespread reports of Iraqi brutality, torture, burning of homes and looting. The population fell by more than a half. Iraq ordered those Kuwaitis still in the country to assume Iraqi citizenship. Events moved fast. Iraq said it had been "invited" in, formed a Quisling government and then annexed Kuwait. Iraqi forces seemed poised to move south and occupy the main oil-producing region of Saudi Arabia, but hesitated. Saudi Arabia's King Fahd asked America to help and President Bush sent in American troops, who were followed by European, Egyptian and other contingents.

The liberation

In November 1990 the Security Council authorised the use of "all necessary means" to liberate Kuwait. Iraq was given until January 15th to start withdrawing and complying with other demands. The anti-Iraqi "coalition", as it came to be known, was formed under American leadership with close co-operation from Saudi Arabia, Egypt and Western Europe. On January 17th 1991 the coalition forces started bombing Iraq. Seven days later these forces entered Kuwait and the Iraqis fled, having first set light to as many of the 1,080 oil wells as they could. The coalition forces pursued them for a short distance but President Bush chose not to send his troops north to take Baghdad. He concluded that his mandate from the Security Council and America's own national interest coincided: it was enough to liberate Kuwait; it would be far too messy to take over Iraq without international approval. The Iraqi leader agreed to the Security Council demands and on February 28th America announced a ceasefire. The war was over: a triumph for governments which decided to prevent the takeover of one country by another, especially if the victim was a rich, oil-producing one. In 1993 Kuwait's bill for reparations that Iraq would have to pay stood at $94 billion.

Ethnic cleansing

The ethnic Kuwaitis obtained the impression, during the occupation, that it was supported by the resident Iraqis, Palestinians and Bedoons. This impression was strengthened, as far as the Palestinians were concerned, when

Yasser Arafat, chairman of the Palestine Liberation Organisation, seemed to support Iraq's grab of Kuwait. So after liberation the Kuwaitis took their revenge. According to the New York-based Human Rights Watch, the amir adopted "policies aimed at eventually expelling from Kuwait nearly all of its remaining Iraqi, Palestinian and Bedoon residents, that included arbitrary arrest and detention, torture and ill-treatment of prisoners, arbitrary searches, heavy fines, threats, public humiliation and the denial of employment. During 1993 hundreds were arrested and held in the Talha Deportation Prison where they were given the choice between leaving Kuwait voluntarily or remaining in that over-crowded and makeshift detention facility."

The Bedoons (nomads mostly from Jordan, Iraq and Syria, many of whom had joined the police and army) were accused en masse of helping the Iraqis. They suffered "summary executions, disappearances and torture". The authorities refused to believe that many of these supposed subversives had acted under duress during the brutal Iraqi occupation. Before the war 350,000 Palestinians lived in Kuwait; after it, and the purges, only 25,000 remained. The Kuwaitis also lost the sympathy of world opinion by their notorious bad treatment of their 180,000-odd low-paid domestic servants from the Philippines, Sri Lanka, India and Bangladesh. Some 1,400 Filipina maids fled to their embassy in Kuwait between April 1991 and April 1992.

Politics: Sabah, Sabah & Sabah Inc

At a meeting in Saudi Arabia before the war, the amir had promised that, on his return home, he would be more democratic. So when he returned the democratic pressure built up again. An election was held (with an absurd 82,000 male voters, accounting for 10% of the native population) in October 1992. Women and naturalised citizens did not have the right to vote, nor did the Bedoons. Although the opposition and independent candidates gained a majority of the 50 seats, the amir, Sheikh Jaber al-Ahmed al-Sabah, remained in charge. The crown prince, Sheikh Abdullah al-Salem al Sabah, was prime minister and the Sabah family also controlled the foreign, defence, interior and information ministries. It was not a dictatorship, however. By tradition each succeeding amir comes from two alternating branches of the Sabah family, descended from the two sons of Sheikh Mubarak, who ruled at the turn of the century.

Originally the Sabahs were the first among equals in relation to the state's powerful merchant families. After the

Sabahs got their hands on Kuwait's vast oil revenues, however, an unwritten understanding developed under which they spread the wealth to the oligarchy. This worked until the collapse of the unofficial stockmarket in 1982, after which the state was criticised by resentful oligarchs for favouring leading debtors from the Sabah family. The merchants, who still fret about the Sabahs' power, are represented by the powerful Chamber of Commerce.

Quite lively

The rest of the opposition is three-pronged. One prong is the so-called "nationalists", a collection of politicians who favour political pluralism in varying degrees. They are mostly members of the Kuwait Democratic Forum. The other two are religion-based: one is pro-Sunni and the other pro-Shia. Both insist they receive no money from abroad. The government is backed by tribally based politicians and so-called independents. In 1994 the political world was buzzing with allegations concerning reported payoffs at the defence ministry which led to the transfer of defence contracts to the finance ministry. There was also the long-running saga of a former oil minister who faced corruption charges. Both men were Sabahs. Debates over the budget, which has been called an exercise in cosmetics, have been lively; the government has been obliged to reach compromises with the National Assembly

Foreign policy: still worried

During the Iran-Iraq war of 1980–88 Kuwait backed Iraq and, with Saudi Arabia, was said to have lent Iraq $30 billion. Kuwait let Iraq use its oil terminals to export its output. As a result, Iran gave Kuwait a hard time, mainly by attacking Kuwaiti tankers in the Gulf. In 1981 Kuwait and its Gulf friends formed the Gulf Co-operation Council (GCC). It eventually also included Saudi Arabia, Qatar, Bahrain, the United Arab Emirates and Oman. Before the Iraqi invasion, Kuwait tried to hew a middle course between the United States and the Soviet Union and to keep Saudi Arabia, the big brother, at arm's length. After liberation Kuwait had some debts to pay. The Americans were given a ten-year treaty under which they could have access to Kuwaiti ports and airfields and store arms, ammunition and other supplies there. Britain and France, the other leading members of the coalition, obtained similar treaties. Inexplicably Iraqi forces amassed on Kuwait's borders again in 1994 but withdrew when American and British troops arrived. There were also fears that Iraq's eventual return to near-respectability by obeying the UN Security Council would let it loose on the Gulf again.

The economy: rich, but short of cash

Kuwait depends on oil and natural gas, which provide more than 90% of export earnings. Before the Iran-Iraq war and the Iraqi occupation, Kuwait carried on a healthy entrepot trade with both countries. That has halted with Iraq and been much reduced with Iran. Kuwait has also suffered from its expulsion of the Palestinians, who performed many skilled jobs. Government has at times appeared to be weak, or devious. In 1994 it displayed these traits in the budget. It was meant to propose a tough budget after having made numerous statements about the need for a 20% spending cut and higher fees for government services, and possibly some new taxes. But the budget contained a 13% spending increase and projected a deficit 20% bigger than the previous year's. The budget committee chairman accused the government of trying to shift the burden of cutting spending and raising taxes to the Assembly. On the other hand, although the government has made much fuss about its determination to sell off state enterprises, the Assembly's response has sometimes been negative. Plans to privatise the Kuwait Telecommunications Company, for example, were delayed. But the Kuwait Investment Authority claimed it would sell all its shareholdings in local companies by 1999.

A need to reschedule?

The governor of the Central Bank, another member of the Sabah family, put the budget deficit in 1994 at an enormous 19% of GDP. He also revealed that the state sector accounted for a vast 76% of economic activity. He added, surprisingly, that if the deficit persisted, it might be necessary for Kuwait to reschedule payments on its foreign debt. It seemed clear that confidence in the post-war economy had not been restored. Nonetheless, GDP grew by 3% in 1993, inflation was at 0.6% and the trade surplus reached $4 billion. Clearly, Kuwait's economy could be more efficiently run. But with 9.4% of the world's estimated oil reserves and a population of only 1.9m, Kuwaitis were unlikely to suffer many sleepless nights worrying about their economic future.

Total area	17,820 sq km	% agricultural area	...
Capital	Kuwait City	Highest point metres	299
Other cities	Hawalli, Al-Salimiya, Al-Jahra		

The economy

GDP $bn	34.1	GDP per head $	23,350
% av. ann. growth in real GDP 1988–93	-2.3	GDP per head in purchasing power parity $	...

Origins of GDP*	% of total	Components of GDP	% of total
Agriculture	0	Private consumption	48.2
Industry	80.6	Public consumption	29.6
of which:		Investment	15.3
manufacturing	8.6	Exports	49.0
Services	19.4	Imports	-42.1

Production *average annual change 1985–93, %*

Agriculture	...	Manufacturing	...
Industry	...	Services	...

Inflation and exchange rates

Consumer price 1993 av. ann. incr.	0.6%	Dinars per $ av. 1994	0.30
Av. ann. rate 1988–93	5.7%	Dinars per SDR av. 1994	0.43

Balance of payments, reserves, aid and debt

			$bn
Visible exports fob	10.4	Capital balance	-3.2
Visible imports fob	-6.0	Overall balance	-1.5
Trade balance	4.4	Change in reserves	-0.9
Invisible inflows	6.3	Level of reserves end Dec.	4.3
Invisible outflows	-2.9	Foreign debt	21.9
Net transfers	-1.4	as % of GDP	74.6
Current account balance	6.3	Debt service	1.6
as % of GDP	28.3	as % of export earnings	9.0

Principal exports	$m fob	Principal imports	$m cif
Crude oil & refined products	10,003	Manufactured goods	5,371
		Food & beverages	1,058
		Industrial raw materials	613
Total	10,542	Total	7,042

Main export destinations	% of total	Main origins of imports	% of total
Japan	36.4	United States	14.8
South Korea	10.4	Japan	12.6
United States	9.4	France	11.0
Netherlands	9.3	Germany	7.9
Taiwan	6.3	United Kingdom	6.6
United Kingdom	6.7	Italy	5.9

Government
System Nominal constitutional monarchy. Executive power rests with the amir and is exercised through Council of Ministers. National Assembly dissolved July 1986. Elections to a reconstituted assembly were held in 1992.
Main political parties None legally recognised

Climate and topography
Dry desert, intensely hot summers, short, cool winters. Flat to slightly undulating desert plain.

People and society

Population m	1.9	% under 15	36.6
Pop. per sq km	107	% over 65	1.2
% urban	96	No. men per 100 women	130
% av. ann. growth 1987–92	2.4	Human Development Index	80.9
No. households m	...		

Life expectancy		Education	
Men	72 yrs	Spending as % of GDP	...
Women	76 yrs	Mean years of schooling	5.5
Crude birth rate	32	Adult literacy %	73.9
Crude death rate	2	Primary school enrolment %	92
Infant mortality rate	14	Secondary school enrolment %	...
Under-5 mortality rate	17	Tertiary education enrolment %	18

Workforce	% of total	Consumer goods ownership	
Services	73	Telephone mainlines per 1,000	...
Industry	26	Televisions per 100	27.1
Agriculture	1		
% of total population	39		

Ethnic groups	% of total	Religious groups	% of total
Kuwaiti	50	Sunni Muslim	45
Other Arab	35	Shi'a Muslim	30
South Asian	9		

Tourism		Health	
Tourist receipts $m	273	Pop. per doctor	690
		Low birthweight babies % of total	7
		Daily calories % of total requirement	130
		% pop. with access to safe water	100

a 1992.

LEBANON

Total area	10,400 sq km	Population	2.9m
GDP	$4.0bn	GDP per head	$1,363
Capital	Beirut	Other cities	Tripoli, Saida, Tyre

Lebanon is an ancient land full of talented people of different religions and cultural roots living cheek by jowl. In the bright part of its history, it gave the world an example of how this can be done successfully, through tolerance and understanding. In the dark part, Lebanon has been an example of hatred, brutality and destructiveness. It now has the opportunity to show the world its bright side again.

History: it started in 3000BC

The Lebanese are traders *par excellence*, perhaps because they are in part descended from the Phoenicians who settled along what is now the Lebanese coast in about 3000BC, and won a reputation for skill in commerce. The Phoenicians' alphabetic script of 22 letters was used at Byblos (modern Jbail) as early as the 15th century BC. The Lebanese may have invented glassblowing. They may also have been linked to the Canaanites of the Old Testament. Among the attractions of the Levantine coastline were its cedars, pines and fir-trees, all famous around the Mediterranean before, during and after the Roman empire. Kings coveted their wood. Peoples of different parts of the Levant came there, among them the Christians who formed the Maronite church which, while far from Rome, remained loyal to the popes. By the 11th century Muslim sects and the Druzes had also moved in, to be followed by the Crusaders. It was the turn of the Ottoman Turks in 1516, but the skilful local leader, Fakhr ad-Din, established a strong form of local autonomy (1586–1635) allied improbably to the Duke of Tuscany. The Turks eventually prevailed, however, and Fakhr ad-Din was executed. Under the Turks, Mount Lebanon was left to itself.

They had to be separated

But distrust between the Maronites and Druzes living there deteriorated into Druze attacks on Maronites and massacres in 1860. The Turks and the western powers intervened and in 1861 an arrangement was made that Mount Lebanon would be administered by a non-local Ottoman Christian. The end of the first world war brought the collapse of the Ottoman empire and its replacement in the region by the French, who created the state of Lebanon within its present borders in 1920. In the inter-war years Lebanon prospered as a sort of French protectorate. In 1943 the Free French declared Lebanon to be independent, although France kept ultimate power. It was only in 1946 that French troops left. Lebanon was governed by the National Pact, under which the president was a Maronite, the prime minister was a Sunni Muslim and the speaker of parliament was a Shia Muslim. Based on the 1932 census, government jobs were distributed to Maronites and the rest of the population on a 6:5 basis.

The start of the troubles

In 1958 the pro-American President Camille Chamoun was accused by Muslim followers of Egypt's radical President Nasser of rigging an election. Fighting erupted and the American Marines were sent in to restore order. Nine years later, after the Arab-Israeli war, south Lebanon was flooded with Palestinian refugees, radical and armed. The weak government in Beirut could not control them. They launched raids on Israel from the south, which suffered from Israeli reprisals. Thousands of Palestinians who had challenged King Hussein's rule in Jordan, and lost, also came to Lebanon. The Palestinians set up their high command there. It became a state within a state. The Palestinians allied with some of the Lebanese Muslims, and the Maronites became nervous. Street fighting led to a civil war that started in 1975 and lasted 15 years. Part of Beirut was wrecked and the capital was split between Maronites in the east and a mixture of Muslims, Druzes and Palestinians in the west. The fighting seemed endless.

Israel intervenes

To retaliate against guerrilla attacks on its northern frontier, Israel seized land in south Lebanon in 1978 and turned it into a "security zone". The guerrillas persisted and Israel intervened again in 1982, this time on a grand scale. The Israelis wanted to force the Palestine Liberation Organisation (PLO) out of Lebanon for good. They cut through the Lebanese, PLO and Syrian defences and reached the outskirts of Beirut. The controversial two-month siege of West Beirut, including bombing by Israeli aircraft and shelling by Israeli artillery, ended only after the PLO agreed to leave the country, which it did by sea from Beirut harbour. A Maronite friend of Israel, Bashir Gemayel, was elected president, but was promptly assassinated. On September 15th Israeli troops entered Beirut and on the next day Christian militiamen, with the knowledge of the Israelis, massacred the mainly civilian populations of the Sabra and Chatila

Palestinian refugee camps. Gemayel was succeeded by his more moderate brother, Amine. Israel held the south of the country, Syria the north.

The treaty that wasn't

Israeli and Lebanese negotiators agreed on May 17th 1983 to a peace treaty including an Israeli and Syrian withdrawal from Lebanon but, under strong pressure from Syria's President Hafez Assad, Lebanon abrogated it. In 1985 Israel withdrew its forces but left the border area in southern Lebanon in the hands of its own "South Lebanon Army". Syria withdrew some 10,000 troops but left some 25,000 in place. To provide stability in Beirut after the departure of the Israelis, a 5,800-man multinational force with troops from France, Italy, America and Britain was sent in. The Muslims thought it was pro-Christian and, in separate attacks by suicide bombers driving lorry-loads of dynamite, 241 American and 58 French marines were killed in their barracks. The force departed. Fighting between Palestinians loyal to the PLO chairman, Yasser Arafat, and Abu Musa, a pro-Syrian Palestinian, ended with Arafat's men leaving their last Lebanese stronghold, the northern port of Tripoli, by ship for Algeria, Tunisia and North Yemen in 1983. The Lebanese Christians were also divided and in turmoil. Fighting persisted across Beirut's "Green Line" between Muslims and Christians. In the south the moderate Shia militia, Amal, fought with the fundamentalist Hizbullah. Finally, Syrian soldiers appeared on the streets of Beirut.

Peace at last

When President Gemayel stepped down in 1988, parliament could not elect a successor and he named the Christian General Michel Aoun to head an interim government until elections could be held. The general led an unsuccessful campaign to oust the Syrians and, later, one against the Maronites' militia, the Lebanese Forces.

In October 1989 the National Assembly, at an extraordinary meeting in Taif, Saudi Arabia, approved a charter of reconciliation. This took account of a population shift that had put the Muslims in a majority. Executive power was transferred from the (Christian) president to the (Sunni Muslim) prime minister. The prime minister would be appointed by the president but only after consulting with the National Assembly. The Assembly seats would be shared equally by Christians and Muslims. Militias were to be disarmed and disbanded and the Lebanese army was to take greater control of the country.

While this was happening the Syrian army would help for a maximum of two years, when it would withdraw to Lebanon's Bekaa Valley and subsequently leave the country at the request of the Lebanese government. (The army has neither withdrawn nor left, and shows no sign of doing so.) Elias Hrawi, an old Christian friend of Syria, was chosen as president after the first choice was assassinated. General Aoun opposed the Taif agreement but his forces were defeated by the Syrians in 1990. The following year Lebanon accepted Syria as its overlord in a treaty of brotherhood, co-operation and co-ordination and a pact of defence and security.

The hostages

In June 1992 two German hostages were released in Beirut, bringing to an end a long and ugly episode involving Lebanese extremists and their friends in Iran. The hostage-takers seized 99 people, some of whom escaped within hours. More than 30 were held for more than a year, including Britons, Americans, French, Italians, Germans, an Irishman and an Indian. Terry Anderson, an American journalist, spent most time in captivity: more than six years. Terry Waite, representative of the archbishop of Canterbury, was released in November 1991 after nearly five years. Several hostages were killed, including the CIA station chief in Beirut.

Foreign policy: a deal with Israel?

Lebanon's foreign policy is subordinated to Syria's. A peace agreement with Israel would have to be preceded by one between Israel and Syria. Lebanon's national interests were separate: while Syria wanted to be given back the Israeli-occupied Golan Heights, Lebanon wanted to be given back the Israeli-occupied security zone along its southern border. From Lebanon, Israel wanted guarantees that the Lebanese army would take full control of the border area and prevent any further guerrilla attacks. In principle, this seemed possible: the most active guerrilla group, associated with the pro-Iranian Hizbullah, said it was fighting purely to oust the Israelis; when that was done it could lay down its arms. Once the Israelis left, the border might even be opened and road, railway and air services could start.

Although Lebanon is under Syrian influence, it still maintains friendly relations with the United States and West European countries. These countries seem, however, not ready to press for the country's genuine independence and are readier to accept Syrian suzerainty as a means of bringing stability to the country and the region.

Politics: money talks

In the summer of 1993 elections to the National Assembly were held for the first time in 20 years. A majority of the Christians and some Muslim groups boycotted them. The Shia Muslim movements, Amal and Hizbullah, did well; Christian representation was weak. Virtually all candidates were allies or friends of Syria. Lebanon was far from being free and independent. In 1994 Syria had 40,000 troops in the centre, north and east of Lebanon. Opponents of Syrian influence received short shrift in military courts. Publications were kept under fairly strict control by the General Directorate of Public Security. A newspaper which said the government would introduce Islamic law was closed. It may have been neo-colonialism, but at least it meant peace.

The old families still matter

Nonetheless, Lebanese politics is still closely tied up with families. Many of the Maronite family leaders, such as ex-President Gemayel, Dory Chamoun and Raymond Eddé, have gone into voluntary exile. In the Bekaa Valley the Hrawi and Skaff families are on good terms with Syria. Among the Sunni Muslims the Karameh family exerts influence in Tripoli and the Druze leader, Walid Jumblatt, following in his father's footsteps, wields influence in the Chouf mountains close to Beirut, rivalled by the scion of another prominent Druze family, Emir Majid Arslan. The capital was several decades ago dominated by the Christians and the Sunnis; in the mid-1990s the Sunnis had taken second place to the Shia. In the Shia-dominated south no family holds a special position: it is the scene for rivalry between Amal, led by Nabih Berri, and Hizbullah, led by Sheikh Nasrallah.

The economy: enter Mr Lebanon Inc

In October 1992 the Lebanese property tycoon, Rafiq Hariri, who has close connections with the Saudi Arabian royal family and extensive business interests in the kingdom, was elected as prime minister, and Lebanon turned another corner. Mr Hariri does not come from an old family. He admitted, freely and openly, that he would take important decisions only in consultation with Syria. When his cabinet became too obstreperous, Mr Hariri asked the Syrian vice-president to intervene. He did, and the ministers quietened down. Mr Hariri has set about rebuilding the country, with his own investments to the fore. The government has set up a company, Solidere, to knock down damaged buildings in Beirut's business district and rebuild the entire area down to the seafront. It is a remarkable and immensely costly undertaking. Mr Hariri is said to be a leading shareholder. In early 1994 Solidere issued shares to raise $650m for the Beirut project. The issue was over-subscribed, raising $926m. Mr Hariri is also said to have been buying, and developing, properties along the coast and to be a leading shareholder in a television station. As a multimillionaire with close ties to Saudi Arabia, Mr Hariri has some room for manoeuvre in his dealings with the Syrians; but not much.

Hopeful signs

Before the civil war Beirut had been the business centre of the Middle East with efficient and discreet banks and trading houses. Many Arabs from countries with stricter codes of public behaviour liked its tolerant atmosphere. Rich Arabs built second homes there. The country was, by Arab standards, relatively industrialised. With the end of the civil war, could it bounce back? It has understandably taken time for business confidence to be lifted off rock bottom. Rich Arabs have revisited their often-damaged second homes, and decided to wait a little longer before calling in the builders, plumbers and electricians.

Nonetheless, things are looking up. According to central bank figures, demand deposits in Lebanese pounds rose by about 23% in 1993 while other deposits rose by 31%. Foreign currency deposits increased from $7.4 billion in 1992 to $9.7 billion in 1993. GDP grew by about 7% in 1993; private investment was up by 21%; and the Lebanese pound gained 7% against the dollar. In early 1994 the central bank had a healthy (for Lebanon) $6.5 billion in foreign exchange and gold reserves. There was a plan to reopen the stockmarket. Telephone, electricity, water and road networks were being upgraded. Beirut harbour and airport were being expanded. A free-trade zone was to be established. The trade figures, on the other hand, revealed the extent of the damage Lebanon has suffered: imports in 1993 amounted to over $3 billion while exports, by one rough estimate, were less than $700m. If the Lebanese stayed on their course, they could once again deploy their Phoenician business skills to their considerable advantage, especially after a peace agreement with Israel. They could also restore their battered reputation for tolerance and understanding.

Total area	10,400 sq km	% agricultural area	30
Capital	Beirut	Highest point metres	Qurnat as-
Other cities	Tripoli, Saida, Tyre		Sawda 3,088
		Main rivers	Litani, Orontes, Kabir

The economy

GDP $bn	4.0	GDP per head $	1,363
% av. ann. growth in		GDP per head in purchasing	
real GDP 1985–93	...	power parity $	...

Origins of GDP*	% of total	Components of GDP	% of total
Agriculture	12.6	Private consumption	106.9
Industry	28.5	Public consumption	15.9
of which:		Investment	23.8
manufacturing	18.5	Exports	20.1
Services	58.9	Imports	66.8

Production *average annual change 1985–93, %*

Agriculture	...	Manufacturing	...
Industry	...	Services	...

Inflation and exchange rates

Consumer price 1993 av. ann. incr.	18.0%	Pounds per $ av. 1994	1,695.20
Av. ann. rate 1988–93	...	Pounds per SDR av. 1994	2,419.03

Balance of payments, reserves, aid and debt

			$bn
Visible exports fob	...	Capital balance	...
Visible imports fob	...	Overall balance	...
Trade balance	...	Change in reserves	...
Invisible inflows	...	Level of reserves end Dec.	2.3
Invisible outflows	...	Foreign debt	...
Net transfers	...	as % of GDP	...
Current account balance	...	Debt service	...
as % of GDP	...	as % of export earnings	...

Principal exports	$m fob	Principal imports*	$m cif
Textiles	126	Consumer goods	1,331
Machinery & appliances	114	Machinery & transport	
Food & beverages	87	equipment	1,165
Metal products	75	Petroleum products	665
Jewellery	67		
Total	686	Total	3,327

Main export destinations	% of total	Main origins of imports	% of total
Saudi Arabia	13.3	Italy	12.7
Syria	11.8	United States	10.6
UAE	9.1	Germany	9.3
France	6.0	France	8.6
Kuwait	5.8	Syria	5.0
Jordan	5.3	United Kingdom	4.4

Government
System Republic. Executive branch composed of president, prime minister and cabinet. Unicameral National Assembly with equal numbers of Christians and Muslims.
Main political parties Amal, Hizbullah, Kataib Party, National Liberal Party, National Bloc, Progressive Socialist Party (Druze)

Climate and topography
Mediterranean. Mild to cool, wet winters and hot, dry summers.

People and society

Population m	2.9	% under 15	34.5
Pop. per sq km	286	% over 65	5.4
% urban	85	No. men per 100 women	92
% av. ann. growth 1987–92	0.8	Human Development Index	60
No. households m	...		

Life expectancy		Education	
Men	66 yrs	Spending as % of GDP	...
Women	71 yrs	Mean years of schooling	4.4
Crude birth rate	28	Adult literacy %	81.3
Crude death rate	7	Primary school enrolment %	112
Infant mortality rate	43	Secondary school enrolment %	...
Under-5 mortality rate	45	Tertiary education enrolment %	...

Workforce	% of total	Consumer goods ownership	
Services	59	Telephone mainlines per 1,000	...
Industry	27	Televisions per 100	32.5
Agriculture	14		
% of total population	30		

Ethnic groups	% of total	Religious groups	% of total
Arab	95	Muslim	75
Armenian	4	Christian	25
Other	1		

Tourism		Health	
Tourist receipts $m	...	Pop. per doctor	670
		Low birthweight babies	
		% of total	10
		Daily calories % of total	
		requirement	129
		% pop. with access to safe water	98

a 1992.

LIBYA

Total area	1,759,540 sq km	Population	4.9m
GDP	$23.5bn	GDP per head	$4,682
Capital	Tripoli	Other cities	Benghazi, Misurata

But for one man, Libya would be a little-noticed country like its neighbour, Tunisia. Thanks to Colonel Muammar Qaddafi it has achieved international notoriety. The "leader of the revolution" is an unpredictable man of seeming contradictions: ready to impose a dictatorship and make use of terrorism yet concerned with social justice; a man of the desert ready to spread revolution around the world; given to making tactical u-turns yet ready to work out his own unorthodox long-term philosophy of government. This mercurial personality, regarded as something of a "mad dog" by his western and Arab contemporaries, has landed his country in uncomfortable isolation. Libya has so much oil money that the UN embargoes imposed on it seem to have had little impact. Tripoli is still buzzing with businessmen. One of the world's biggest civil engineering projects, the Great Man-Made River, to bring water by pipeline from aquifers under the Sahara desert to Tripoli and Benghazi, is well under way. But time for the colonel may be running out.

History: a time for invaders

This ancient land has been invaded by Phoenicians, Numidians, Greeks, Romans, Vandals and Byzantines. They were followed in 648 by Arabs, who ran the place until Spain took over in 1510, followed by the Turks in 1551. The Turks gave way to the local Karamanli dynasty from 1711 until 1835, and then reasserted themselves. From 1870 to 1911 the area was dominated by the Sanusi religious order. But the Turks and Italians could not be kept in check. Before the first world war an Italian invading force had taken control of the coastal towns while the Turks had signed up the local authorities in the interior in an alliance against the Italians. After the war the Italians began to pacify the country. They completed the job after capturing the Libyan nationalist hero, Omar Mukhtar, and hanging him in 1931.

Short-lived triumph

Italy's colonisation lasted until 1942 when its soldiers, alongside the Germans, lost the war in the Western Desert. The British took over Tripolitania and Cyrenaica while the French took over the Fezzan. After the war the two ran Libya uneventfully until 1951, when they granted it independence under King Idris (originally Muhammad Idris al-

Sanusi, a member of the Sanusi religious order and a resistance hero). The leaders of the new country fell into disagreements. Some wanted government to be devolved to the provinces while others called for centralisation. Some did not like the king's right to introduce and veto legislation and to nominate 12 of the 24 members of the senate. Libya was dominated by some elite families and advisers from Britain and the United States, which set up big military bases. Libya made a modest living by exporting esparto grass and scrap metal from second world war battlefields.

Then everything changed

By 1960 substantial deposits of oil had been discovered. By 1966 exports amounted to 70m tons a year. Sudden wealth led to corruption, which spread and brought discontent. Egyptian Nasserism, with its heady blend of nationalism, socialism and xenophobia, was in the ascendant in the Arab world. Libya was ripe for change. On September 1st 1969 the unknown 28-year-old Captain Qaddafi seized power while the king was holidaying in Egypt and proclaimed Libya to be a republic ruled by a revolutionary council. British and American forces left in 1970. Colonel Qaddafi, as he had promoted himself, set up the monolithic General People's Congress in 1977 and the country was renamed the Great Socialist People's Libyan Arab Jamahiriya.

Libya was run according to the tenets of Qaddafi's Third Universal Theory, as enunciated in his Green Book. He rejected parliamentary democracy and capitalism. He wanted workers to be "partners not wage earners" and (perhaps harking back to his roots in the desert) envisaged an era when money would be replaced by barter. Local government was handled by Basic People's Congresses at which decisions were made "by the masses" yet without a vote. But Colonel Qaddafi and his sidekick, Staff-Major Abdusalam Jalloud, ruled supreme. There was no hint of western-style democracy. Qaddafi kept control through his murky revolutionary committees made up of hand-picked young men blindly obedient to the Leader of the Revolution. They passed the word from on high to the Basic People's Congresses, which did what they were told.

Generous brutality

Signs in English were taken down. Alcohol was banned. Most shops and bazaars were closed. People were told to use state supermarkets. But there were advantages. Colonel Qaddafi ordered the construction of much public housing. Jobs were easy to find because the government was swimming in oil money. Immigrants did all the dirty work. Many Libyans became lazy and enjoyed the good life. Public services worked reasonably well.

Politics: watch your back

In the 1970s Libya appeared to adopt a policy of eliminating dissidents living abroad, whom the regime called "stray dogs". Twenty-five exiles died in 37 attacks. In 1993 a Libyan who had taken part in a meeting of dissidents in Geneva subsequently disappeared from his hotel in Cairo. Opposition groups were, however, no threat. They were divided and ineffectual. The best known is the National Front for the Salvation of Libya, founded in 1981 by Muhammad Megharief, which has a military wing called the Libyan National Army. Its men were said to have been trained by the American Central Intelligence Agency, but never to have fought against government forces. A coup attempt in October 1993 failed apparently because the regime was tipped off; about 1,500 people were detained. However, disaffection among the tribes of the interior was escalating.

Foreign policy: marry me

Colonel Qaddafi has sought unity with a number of Arab countries. In 1969 he arranged a federation with Egypt and Sudan. Nothing came of it. In 1972 an alliance with Egypt was mooted but never implemented. The colonel signed up with Tunisia in 1974 and Syria in 1980 but nothing came of it. An agreement with Chad, to the south, in 1981 led to the discreet arrival of the Libyan army in that country. It was subsequently asked to leave and did so. In 1984 Morocco's King Hassan surprised the world by signing up with Libya.

Why did these leaders go along with the unpredictable colonel? Possibly because he crossed their palms with silver. Perhaps, some suggest, because he can be almost hypnotically persuasive in private meetings. Most probably the partners signed up for some for political advantage (his deal with Morocco included a promise to stop aiding Morocco's Polisario rebels). Impecunious African presidents have taken a different tack: they make the pilgrimage to Tripoli, praise the Leader and go home not with a unity pact but with a handsome cheque.

Kill them

The colonel's most disagreeable behaviour has been his support for terrorism. He has sent aid to the Irish Republican Army (yet subsequently co-operated with Britain in providing information about it) and the Touareg rebels in Niger and Mali. He is said to have given sanctuary to two arch-terrorists, "Carlos" and Abu Nidal. He is consumed by a hatred for Israel, which he calls the "Zionist entity". Mysteriously, the most popular and respected imam of the Lebanese Shia Muslims, Moussa Badr, disappeared while in Libya and many Lebanese blamed the colonel.

In 1984 a British policewoman was killed by a shot fired from inside the Libyan embassy in London. Libya was accused of complicity in the hijacking of the cruise ship *Achille Lauro* and a TWA airliner in 1985 and, a year later, shootings in Rome and Vienna airports and a bomb attack on a Berlin nightclub frequented by American servicemen. On thin evidence the Americans retaliated by bombing Tripoli and Benghazi.

Right or wrong, however, the raids seemed to have stopped Libyan-inspired terrorism. Until, that is, the cases of the Pan Am airliner which crashed in Lockerbie, Scotland, in 1988 after a bomb on board exploded and the French UTA airliner which blew up over Niger in 1989. Attempts to bring Libyan suspects to justice failed when Colonel Qaddafi refused to hand them over. The UN Security Council imposed sanctions, banning international airline flights to and from Libya and imposing an embargo on arms and spare parts. In 1993 the Council tightened the sanctions with, among other things, a freeze on Libyan overseas financial assets.

The economy: oil, oil and more oil

Hydrocarbons account for a third of national output but generate more than 95% of vital foreign exchange earnings. Libya's isolation and the relatively low world oil price led to a fall in GDP in 1993 of 4.5%; a similar fall was predicted for 1994. GDP was expected to perk up in 1995. But Libya was in trouble. Even with all its oil and its small population (4.9m), Libya runs a trade deficit. In 1993 it had a current-account deficit of $2.3 billion and was expected to have ones of about $1.6–1.7 billion in 1994 and 1995. It had precious few capital inflows to cover these deficits and must be using up its reserves. Before the UN financial sanctions went into effect, Libya had foreign exchange reserves excluding gold of only about $6.2 billion. The other measure it is clearly taking is to cut imports drastically. Inflation will rise. The regime is heading for more unpopularity.

Total area	1,759,540 sq km	% agricultural area	1
Capital	Tripoli	Highest point metres	Picco Bette
Other cities	Benghazi, Misurata		2,286
		Main rivers	none

The economy

GDP $bn	23.5	GDP per head $	4,682
% av. ann. growth in		GDP per head in purchasing	
real GDP 1985–93	...	power parity $	...

Origins of GDP[a]	% of total	Components of GDP[a]	% of total
Agriculture	4.5	Private consumption	45
Industry	49.7	Public consumption	28
of which:		Investment	20
manufacturing	11.0	Exports	50
Services	45.8	Imports	-43

Production average annual change 1985–93, %

Agriculture	...	Manufacturing	...
Industry	...	Services	...

Inflation and exchange rates

Consumer price 1993 av. ann. incr.	...	Dinars per $ av. 1994	0.32
Av. ann. rate 1988–93	...	Dinars per SDR av. 1994	0.46

Balance of payments, reserves, aid and debt

			$bn
Visible exports fob	7.7	Capital balance	1.5
Visible imports fob	-8.2	Overall balance	0.2
Trade balance	-0.6	Change in reserves	-1.2
Invisible inflows	0.8	Level of reserves end Dec.	5.2
Invisible outflows	-2.0	Foreign debt	5.7
Net transfers	-0.5	as % of GDP	24.3
Current account balance	-2.3	Debt service	0.9
as % of GDP	-9.6	as % of export earnings	10.1

Principal exports[a]	$m fob	Principal imports[a]	$m cif
Oil & derivatives	9,480	Oil & derivatives	1,500
		Others	6,600
Total	9.970	Total	8,100

Main export destinations	% of total	Main origins of imports	% of total
Italy	37.7	Italy	23.9
Germany	17.9	Germany	16.3
Spain	10.2	United Kingdom	8.7
Turkey	5.6	France	7.2
France	4.9	Turkey	5.6
Greece	4.8	Netherlands	4.8

Government

System People's republic headed, although he holds no official post, by Colonel Qaddafi as "Leader of the Revolution". Local people's congresses form an electoral base for the General People's Congress.
Main political parties No official parties

Climate and topography

Mediterranean along coast. Extremely dry interior. Mostly barren and flat with some plateaus and depressions.

People and society

Population m	4.9	% under 15	48.3
Pop. per sq km	3	% over 65	2.3
% urban	84	No. men per 100 women	104
% av. ann. growth 1987–92	4.2	Human Development Index	70.3
No. households m	...		

Life expectancy		Education	
Men	66 yrs	Spending as % of GDP	...
Women	71 yrs	Mean years of schooling	3.5
Crude birth rate	36	Adult literacy %	66.5
Crude death rate	6	Primary school enrolment %	...
Infant mortality rate	60	Secondary school enrolment %	...
Under-5 mortality rate	105	Tertiary education enrolment %	...

Workforce	% of total	Consumer goods ownership	
Services	50	Telephone mainlines per 1,000	...
Industry	30	Televisions per 100	9.9
Agriculture	20		
% of total population	24		

Ethnic groups	% of total	Religious groups	% of total
Berber-Arab	97	Sunni Muslim	97
European	3		

Tourism		Health	
Tourist receipts $m	6	Pop. per doctor	690
		Low birthweight babies	
		% of total	5
		Daily calories % of total	
		requirement	140
		% pop. with access to safe water	93

a 1992.

MOROCCO

Total area	458,730 sq km	Population	26.7m
GDP	$27.6bn	GDP per head	$1,030
Capital	Rabat	Other cities	Casablanca, Fez, Marrakesh

Morocco is one of the most stable countries in the Arab world. But it has the potential for internal religious conflict. Its relative calm has been achieved through the skill of King Hassan, a politician to his fingertips.

History: short dynasties, long occupations

Morocco's early history reached high points under Idris (788–985), a descendant of the Prophet Muhammad, and two religious movements, the Almoravids and the Almohads, whose power in the 12th century stretched at one point from Spain to what is now Libya. The Almohads were succeeded by the Merinids and an era in which there were alternating periods of anarchy and prosperity, as Berber tribes clashed with intruding Arab tribes and also with Spanish and Portuguese colonists on the Mediterranean and Atlantic coasts. In 1664 the Sultan Rashid II of the House of Alawi (which remains Morocco's royal family) brought a temporary period of peace and prosperity. But in the 19th century European governments began to be attracted by North Africa. The French took Algiers in 1830. Spain asserted its influence over the Atlantic coast south of Casablanca (an area that would later be known as the Spanish Sahara and spark rebellion). Morocco was split into two zones of influence, French in the north and Spanish in the south, in 1904. The French took precedence, however, and Morocco became a French protectorate with a resident-general in 1912. France, Spain and Britain set up the international zone of Tangier in 1923.

The colonists withdraw

It took time for the French to pacify Morocco. A rebellion by the renowned Abdel Krim in 1921 was quelled only in 1926. By the outbreak of the second world war Morocco was pacified, although nationalist sentiment was growing. It was only in 1956, however, that independence was granted by France and Spain. The sultan, Sidi Muhammad ben Youssef, adopted the title of King Muhammad V. Tangier became Moroccan again. Spain handed back the enclave of Ifni in 1959 but kept two others, Ceuta and Melilla. It withdrew in 1975 from the Spanish (or Western) Sahara, which was split a year later between Morocco and Mauritania. The Mauritanians gave up their share in 1979 and it was added to Morocco's bit. Led by the king, hundreds of thousands of Moroccans moved into the Spanish Sahara in the so-called Green March. This annoyed the local Polisario nationalists, who wanted the ex-colony to become independent. A long desert war ensued between Morocco and the rebels, who were backed by Algeria. At great expense the king built a defensive wall to keep the Polisario out and by 1994 it was protecting four-fifths of the territory. A UN-sponsored referendum on the future of the territory was repeatedly postponed.

Politics: Always Hassan

King Hassan succeeded his father on his death in 1961. Displaying remarkable skill, he managed to dominate the country while giving politicians and unionists a limited amount of freedom. There was the conservative Istiqlal (Independence) Party, founded in 1943, which wanted to reduce royal power. The radical National Union of Popular Forces (UNFP) broke away from Istiqlal in 1959 and split itself in 1974 with the formation of the Socialist Union of Popular Forces (USFP). Various parties and local government leaders were loyal to the king. This political effervescence failed to satisfy everybody and the king survived two attempted coups in 1971 and 1972. In response he turned populist and announced several nationalisations. Some politicians and unionists who had been detained were released as human rights became an increasingly important issue. Elections were held with the usual complaints of fraud and a muzzled press.

Nonetheless, Morocco's fragile and imperfect version of Arab democracy was consolidated. Prime ministers came and went, trying to deal with the country's budget deficit and debating the benefits of privatisation. Unions protested against low wages and price increases (over a third of the 26.3m population lives below the poverty line; half the population is under the age of 20; most graduates cannot find jobs). Vigorous debates were held in the 333-seat, one chamber legislature. Deputies for 111 seats are elected by local governments and the remainder are elected directly. Behind the scenes, discreetly exercising ultimate power, was the king, who had the right to hire and fire prime ministers and call elections and who played off rival parties against each other as they competed for patronage and power.

Strong views

In the general election of 1993 some 2,000 candidates stood

for one of 11 parties or as independents. It produced a hung parliament. After failing to persuade the opposition to form a minority government, the king asked Mohammed Karim Lamrani, an urbane royalist, to serve as prime minister of a government of technocrats. He was succeeded in May 1994 by Abdellatif Filali, a veteran diplomat whose son is married to one of the king's daughters. One reason for the opposition's refusal to form a government is the king's insistence that his tough and feared interior minister, Driss Basri, should remain at his post. In addition to running the police and the jails, Basri has been the king's intelligence chief. The opposition, led by Istiqlal and the USFP, denounced the unelected technocratic government as anti-democratic and attacked it for failing to resolve the problems of unemployment, poverty, poor schools, and inadequate healthcare and low-cost housing. But it was unable to come up with viable alternatives, and the king's programme won parliamentary approval in 1994 with the support of parliamentary independents.

Society: will the Islamists erupt?

The key to the king's survival is his success in smothering Islamic fundamentalism. So far he has done this with great skill. On one hand, he outdid the fundamentalists in their zeal by building, in Casablanca, the biggest mosque in the world. He also claims to be a descendant of the Prophet Muhammad. His title is "Commander of the Faithful". He may be criticised for the corruption of the royal family and squandering money on royal palaces scattered around the country, but he cannot be faulted on purely religious grounds. On the other hand, extremism has been spreading, and the king has dealt with it in a low-key way.

There are 13 known Islamic groups in Morocco, all of which are banned from politics. The leader of one, Abdessalem Yassine, has been under house arrest since 1989. A founder of this group was jailed for two years. He said: "If things in this country continue as they are, Morocco could have the same problems as Algeria." The leader of another extremist group said: "Everyone knows the king runs a clever police state. But eventually the Islamists will take over. It is inevitable." But is it? Few Moroccans want the tragic experience of next-door Algeria. A kind of democracy is in place and being consolidated. It might even be improved. There is no serious ethnic strife. At least a third of the population are Berbers. But the definition of this group is difficult since it refers to fluency in a Berber language. Many Moroccans are fluent in Arabic and one of the Berber languages.

Foreign policy: subtle yet daring

For a man concerned with survival, the king has taken risks. He marched into the old Spanish Sahara and got away with it. He has held secret meetings with Israeli leaders, most notably Shimon Peres. He kept fairly good relations with France, marred by the disappearance and apparent kidnapping of a radical opposition leader, Ben Barka, on a Paris street in 1965. Relations with the United States have mostly been excellent; the king was seen as a cold war ally and he contributed 1,000 soldiers to the coalition force in the Gulf war against Iraq. But in 1984 he baffled his American friends by signing a "unity" agreement with Libya's Colonel Muammar Qaddafi. There was logic in this odd action. Morocco has always been a rival for leadership of North Africa with Algeria, which financed, supplied and armed the Polisario rebels. Algeria formed an alliance with Tunisia and Mauritania in 1983, isolating Morocco. The king's pact with the colonel counter-balanced it. As a fringe benefit Libya stopped helping the Polisario. The pact eventually faded.

The economy: secret of survival

The government has slowly been putting into place, with some ups and downs, an IMF-style economic reform including fiscal caution and privatisation. Mindful of political trouble from widespread redundancies at state enterprises, however, it is moving cautiously. Morocco's dependency on phosphates is lessening as other sectors of the economy, such as manufacturing, perk up. GDP growth was projected by independent analysts at about 5% for 1994 and 1995 (the population is growing at 2.2% a year). Inflation in 1994 was roughly 7%. Morocco's trade deficit ($2.4 billion in 1993) is caused by the country's dependence on imported fuel and food but is partly covered by tourist income and remittances by overseas Moroccans (about 1.7m Moroccans have emigrated in search of a better life; more than 80% are in Europe and of them 42% are in France).

There will be no return to the heavy deficit spending of the early 1980s. For all his imperfections, King Hassan has planted the seeds of stable economic progress with more than a dash of democracy. It should be enough to keep the fundamentalists at bay.

Total area	458,730 sq km	% agricultural area	19
Capital	Rabat	Highest point metres	Toubkal 4,165
Other cities	Casablanca, Fez, Marrakesh	Main rivers	Sebou, Oum er-Rbia, Moulouya

The economy

GDP $bn	27.6	GDP per head $	1,030
% av. ann. growth in real GDP 1985–93	2.9	GDP per head in purchasing power parity $	3,270

Origins of GDP	% of total	Components of GDP	% of total
Agriculture	14.3	Private consumption	66.0
Industry	32.4	Public consumption	18.2
of which:		Investment	21.2
manufacturing	18.0	Exports	22.5
Services	53.3	Imports	-27.9

Production average annual change 1985–93, %

Agriculture	0.6	Manufacturing	3.7
Industry	2.9	Services	4.1

Inflation and exchange rates

Consumer price 1993 av. ann. incr.	5.2%	Dirhams per $ av. 1994	9.20
Av. ann. rate 1988–93	5.8%	Dirhams per SDR av. 1994	13.14

Balance of payments, reserves, aid and debt $bn

Visible exports fob	3.7	Capital balance	0.9
Visible imports fob	-6.1	Overall balance	0.1
Trade balance	-2.4	Change in reserves	0.2
Invisible inflows	2.6	Level of reserves end Dec.	3.7
Invisible outflows	-3.0	Foreign debt	21.4
Net transfers	2.3	as % of GDP	81.7
Current account balance	-0.5	Debt service	2.6
as % of GDP	-1.9	as % of export earnings	30.7

Principal exports	$m fob	Principal imports	$m cif
Consumer goods	1,062	Industrial & agricultural	
Food, drink & tobacco	962	equipment	1,831
Semi-finished goods	900	Semi-manufactures	1,513
Mineral ores	375	Energy	965
Capital goods	183	Food, drink & tobacco	956
		Consumer goods	724
Total	3,682	Total	6,062

Main export destinations	% of total	Main origins of imports	% of total
France	34.7	France	29.9
Germany	9.9	Spain	9.2
Spain	7.8	Germany	8.0
Italy	5.6	United States	7.7
Japan	4.9	Italy	6.7

Government
System Constitutional monarchy. Prime minister and cabinet are appointed by king. Legislature is unicameral Chamber of Representatives.
Main political parties Union Constitutionelle, Istiqlal, Union Socialiste des Forces Populaires, Mouvement Populaire, Rassemblement National des Indépendants, Mouvement National Populaire, Parti National Démocrate, Parti du Progrès et du Socialisme, Organisation de l'Action Démocratique et Populaire

Climate and topography
Mediterranean, with wider extremes in the interior. Mostly mountains with coastal plains. Desert in the south.

People and society
Population m	26.7	% under 15	38.7
Pop. per sq km	59	% over 65	3.9
% urban	47	No. men per 100 women	100
% av. ann. growth 1987–92	2.2	Human Development Index	54.9
No. households m	3.4		

Life expectancy
		Education	
Men	64 yrs	Spending as % of GDP	…
Women	68 yrs	Mean years of schooling	3
Crude birth rate	26	Adult literacy %	52.5
Crude death rate	7	Primary school enrolment %	66
Infant mortality rate	57	Secondary school enrolment %	28
Under-5 mortality rate	84	Tertiary education enrolment %	10

Workforce	% of total	Consumer goods ownership	
Services	29	Telephone mainlines per 1,000	16
Industry	25	Televisions per 100	7.4
Agriculture	46		
% of total population	33		

Ethnic groups	% of total	Religious groups	% of total
Arab-Berber	99	Muslim	98
Non-Moroccan	1	Christian	1

Tourism		Health	
Tourist receipts $m	1,360	Pop. per doctor	4,840
		Low birthweight babies % of total	9
		Daily calories % of total requirement	131
		% pop. with access to safe water	56

OMAN

Total area	212,460 sq km	Population	1.6m
GDP	$9.6bn	GDP per head	$5,600
Capital	Muscat	Other cities	Salalah, Nazwa

Once an under-developed backwater, Oman is being rapidly modernised. Built on income from oil and, more recently, natural gas, it looks fairly prosperous. But despite its riches it runs a current-account deficit and its oil reserves are ebbing away. There is ample natural gas, however; it may even be delivered to India by a pipeline.

History: adventurous

Oman's history goes back to the third millenium BC when copper is thought to have been exported by Oman to present-day Iraq and towns such as Ur of the Chaldees. Intrepid mariners and traders discovered Oman as it was on their routes to the East. The Romans put it on their maps and bought frankincense, spice, sandalwood and thoroughbred horses there. The Omanis were converted early to a tolerant form of Islam. They could speak their minds freely: their country was well off the beaten track.

In the 16th century the Portuguese established themselves on the coast and built two great fortresses there. But in 1650 Imam Nasser expelled them. This was a prosperous time for the Omanis, who had always been an adventurous people (an Omani served as a guide for the Portuguese master-mariner, Vasco da Gama). Muscat, the capital, became a centre of the slave trade. The Omanis ousted the Portuguese from what are now Zanzibar, Mogadishu and Mombasa. After a period of civil war in the 18th century, Ahmad ibn Said became imam and started a dynasty which still rules Oman: the Albusaidi. Though Oman's population was small, Ahmad and one of his successors, Said bin Sultan, established the country as a coherent state and signed an agreement with the British in 1839. The country was divided into three regions: Muscat, to the north, Oman, in the centre, and Dhofar, in the south. (After independence recognised by the British in 1951, the country was called the Sultanate of Muscat and Oman; in 1970 its name was changed to the Sultanate of Oman.)

Muscat against Oman

Serious trouble first came to the country in 1913 when a rebellion erupted in Oman's interior against rule from Muscat. The Oman region was ruled by an imam, Muscat by a sultan. The dispute was patched up by granting some autonomy to the rebellious tribes supporting the imam. But in 1955 the sultan's forces took over the imam's towns and the imam lost power. From 1957 to 1959, however, his brother organised guerrilla warfare, and the sultan sought and obtained British help. Sultan Said bin-Taimur (1932–70) was deeply unpopular and a painful embarrassment to British agents protecting their country's interest in the area. He tolerated slavery and spent his money mostly on guns.

The British feared the sultanate could be ripe for a leftist revolution. A rebellion erupted in southern Dhofar in 1964 under the Popular Front for the Liberation of Oman. The British could see the writing on the wall and the sultan was duly deposed in 1970. His son, Qaboos, a 30-year-old Sandhurst graduate who wanted to transform the country with its oil revenues, took over. His appointment gave an impulse to Oman's hopes for international recognition as an independent state rather than a British protectorate; a year later it was admitted to the UN. The rebellion dragged on but Qaboos was aided by several Arab countries, Iran, India and Pakistan in addition to Britain, while the rebels were aided only by South Yemen. In 1975 Qaboos declared that the insurgency was over. It was only in 1982 that Oman and South Yemen established diplomatic relations; a border agreement with united Yemen was signed in 1992.

Politics: not exactly democratic

In 1981 Qaboos set up a Consultative Council made up of businessmen, government officials and regional representatives, to which 19 more government officials were added in 1983. Its power was limited to commenting on developments and making recommendations. In 1990 he set up a Consultative Council (*majlis al-shur*) to which cabinet ministers would report. It had no legislative power, however. Its sessions are televised and have a wide audience. Criticism of the government, and particularly of the sultan, is not tolerated. But exchanges between members, and between members and ministers, are often the main topic of discussion in Muscat cafes and among the elite.

Foreign policy: firmly pro-western

With his personal British connections, his British military and political advisers and British officers commanding many of his troops, it is not surprising that Qaboos acquired a reputation for being an Anglophile and, during the cold war, pro-western. Oman was used for American military exercises and to store American supplies. Oman was particularly important during the Iran-Iraq war because it controlled an enclave on the peninsula at the southern side of the Strait of Hormuz (Iran controlled the northern side). The Americans are said to have upgraded Omani installations for use in the event of a wider war in the Gulf. Masirah island was particularly important.

Oman is a member of the Gulf Co-operation Council and a strong proponent of military co-operation. At the same time, however, it preserved unusually good relations with Iran, its close neighbour across the Gulf. Qaboos sometimes saw Oman as a mediator between Iran and Iraq, and Omanis are believed to have carried messages to Iran for interested parties. Under Qaboos relations between Oman and South Yemen improved and did better when South Yemen united with North Yemen. The south's rebellion against northern preponderance in 1994 caused acute concern in Oman. The flight of the southern leader and Yemeni vice-president, Ali Salim al-Baidh, to Oman was an embarrassment. But Mr al-Baidh promised to abandon politics. In 1992 the Omani armed forces numbered 23,000 soldiers, 3,000 sailors and 3,500 airmen with 6,000 servicemen in the royal household. The navy's fast-attack craft patrol the Strait of Hormuz and the Gulf of Oman.

Society: oil corrupts

Oman's oil money has tended to corrupt the population. Many Omanis have not sought high qualifications to deal with the high-tech world; they often let immigrants run the shops and they disdain jobs such as street-cleaning. Qaboos is looking to the future when oil and gas will not bring in enough money to support the fast-growing population of foreigners and has launched his "Omanisation" programme: foreigners owning market stalls have been told to close down, and Omanis are said to be sweeping the streets which are, uncharacteristically for this part of the world, spotlessly clean. In 1993 expatriate workers made up roughly 65% of the workforce.

Until 1994 there had been little sign of Islamic extremism. Most of the indigenous population are relatively liberal Ibadhi Muslims; about a quarter are Sunni. Nonetheless, the arrest of many members of an underground Islamist grouping, mostly Sunni, in May and June 1994, and of more in August, heightened nervousness about extremism in Oman and elsewhere in the Gulf. The government was aware that Oman's wealth had not spread to the inhabitants of remote small towns and villages, which might be the breeding ground for extremism.

The economy: oil is not enough

Despite its oil riches, Oman has been running a current-account deficit. Of the regional oil producers and exporters it comes fifth after Saudi Arabia, Iraq (not exporting owing to UN sanctions), Iran and the United Arab Emirates. But its reserves are fast running out. Natural gas is another matter: in 1994 the government signed a deal with a foreign consortium led by Shell to exploit 7,000 billion cubic feet of proven and recoverable gas reserves. Production is to start in 2000. Total natural gas reserves are officially put at 20 trillion cubic feet. The government has been examining the idea of building an undersea pipeline to take 2 billion cubic feet of natural gas a day to India. Two British companies, Wimpey Environmental and a division of Racal, were asked to check water temperatures, the strength of currents, wave patterns and meteorological conditions along the 1,000km route and to carry out a survey of the seabed.

In the mid-1990s privatisation was under way, including hotels, a cement company and part of a bank. These sales were expected to give some bounce to the Oman stockmarket, which was being opened to foreigners through investment funds. The first one was Oryx, managed by the London-based Blakeney Management.

Time to diversify

Facing growing budget deficits, the government has been scaling down spending and selling bonds to cover what remains. The sultan, anxious to expand the non-oil economy, told his ministers to promote tourism. Conferences on tourism were subsequently held and travel agents have been invited. But more hotels are needed before it will make sense to encourage more holidaymakers. The sultan has also been pressing for an expansion of industry. There were high hopes of selling more manufactured products to neighbouring Yemen, but the eruption of civil war there in 1994 seemed likely to hold back economic growth, and demand for Omani goods, for some time. Agriculture is important but threatened: aquifers are being over-pumped and salt water is seeping into the soil along the coast. The main products are dates, alfalfa, limes, tomatoes, bananas and aubergines. There are about 83,000 camels, 24,000 donkeys, 770,000 goats, 220,000 sheep and 136,000 cattle.

Total area	212,460 sq km	% agricultural area	...
Capital	Muscat	Highest point metres	Jabal ash-
Other cities	Salalah, Nazwa		Sham 3,018

The economy

GDP $bn	9.6	GDP per head $	5,600
% av. ann. growth in		GDP per head in purchasing	
real GDP 1985–93	7.7	power parity $	10,720

Origins of GDP[a]	% of total	Components of GDP[a]	% of total
Agriculture	4.0	Private consumption	39.4
Industry	52.0	Public consumption	36.7
of which:		Investment	18.0
manufacturing	4.0	Exports	5.8
Services	44.0	Imports	-30.0

Production *average annual change 1985–93, %*

Agriculture	7.1	Manufacturing	18.3
Industry	9.6	Services	6.0

Inflation and exchange rates

Consumer price 1993 av. ann. incr.	0.9%	Omani rials per $ av. 1994	0.39
Av. ann. rate 1988–93	...	Omani rials per SDR av. 1994	0.56

Balance of payments, reserves, aid and debt

			$bn
Visible exports fob	5.4	Capital balance	0.1
Visible imports fob	-4.0	Overall balance	-1.1
Trade balance	1.3	Change in reserves	-1.1
Invisible inflows	0.5	Level of reserves end Dec.	1.0
Invisible outflows	-1.5	Foreign debt	2.7
Net transfers	-1.3	as % of GDP	34.9
Current account balance	-1.0	Debt service	0.6
as % of GDP	-8.8	as % of export earnings	11.3

Principal exports[b]	$m fob	Principal imports[a]	$m cif
Oil	4,237	Machinery & transport	
		equipment	1,650
		Manufactured goods	960
		Food & live animals	474
		Chemicals	179
Total	4,871	Total	3,764

Main export destinations	% of total	Main origins of imports	% of total
UAE	33.4	UAE	23.7
Japan	19.5	Japan	20.8
South Korea	14.0	United Kingdom	11.9
China	7.0	United States	6.6
Iran	2.7	France	6.1

Government
System Monarchy with no written constitution. Sultan legislates by decree and rules with the assistance of an appointed Council of Ministers.
Main political parties none

Climate and topography
Hot and humid along coast, dry interior. Vast central desert plain, rugged mountains in north and south.

People and society

Population m	1.6	% under 15	47.1
Pop. per sq km	8	% over 65	2.7
% urban	12	No. men per 100 women	112
% av. ann. growth 1987–92	4.5	Human Development Index	65.4
No. households m	...		

Life expectancy		Education	
Men	68 yrs	Spending as % of GDP	3.5
Women	72 yrs	Mean years of schooling	0.9
Crude birth rate	43	Adult literacy %	35
Crude death rate	5	Primary school enrolment %	100
Infant mortality rate	20	Secondary school enrolment %	57
Under-5 mortality rate	28	Tertiary education enrolment %	6

Workforce	% of total	Consumer goods ownership	
Services	29	Telephone mainlines per 1,000	68
Industry	22	Televisions per 100	75.5
Agriculture	49		
% of total population	28		

Ethnic groups	% of total	Religious groups	% of total
Arab	99	Ibadhi Muslim	75
		Other Muslim	25

Tourism		Health	
Tourist receipts $m	85	Pop. per doctor	1,060
		Low birthweight babies % of total	10
		Daily calories % of total requirement	...
		% pop. with access to safe water	46

a 1992.
b 1991.

PALESTINE

In early 1995 the Palestinians were moving, with stops, starts and hesitations, towards the establishment of their own state comprising most of the West Bank and the Gaza strip. The Middle East peace process had many enemies, on both the Arab and Israeli sides, and the "devil was in the details". But the political will to seize the opportunity remained strong.

History: Britain gave up

The history of the Palestinians is inextricably bound up with that of Israel and Jordan. Palestine was ruled by the Turks until the end of the first world war, when it came under British influence. In 1923 Britain took over the League of Nations mandate to rule Palestine. Jewish immigration gathered momentum; Arab residents protested. By 1948 the Jewish population had reached about 650,000. Militant Jews in the Stern gang and Irgun Zvai Leumi tried to make the mandate unworkable.

The Palestinian exodus

The Irgun Zvai Leumi captured the village of Deir Yassin and killed its inhabitants, an act which spread terror among Palestinians and sparked off an exodus. A UN commission recommended in 1947 the establishment of a Jewish state and set out the boundaries, which included the Mediterranean coastline. The Arabs were outraged. They began fighting the Jews, who began seizing land. In 1947 the British gave up the mandate and transferred Transjordan to the Arabs. The United Nations General Assembly approved a resolution, which became known as the partition plan, providing for Jewish and Palestinian independence by dividing Palestine into two states. The Palestinians and other Arabs rejected it. Nonetheless David Ben Gurion, head of the Jewish Agency, declared the state of Israel in May 1948, on the eve of Britain's withdrawal. Ten minutes later the United States recognised Israel. In the ensuing war of 1948–49 against the armies of Egypt, Syria and Transjordan, and a contingent from Saudi Arabia, Israel gained control of a larger area of Palestine than it had been allocated, including half of the international zone of Jerusalem. Jordan took over the other half, and the West Bank. By the time the mandate had expired 400,000 Palestinians had become refugees; after independence, another 400,000 are said to have fled. The hostility of the Arab world was total. The seeds of Palestinian terrorism were planted.

The PLO is formed

The Palestine National Council, a loose, appointed body including prominent figures living in the West Bank and Gaza strip as well as in the *diaspora*, set up the Palestine Liberation Organisation (PLO) in 1964 with the initial aim of driving the Israeli intruders into the Mediterranean. By 1974 it was so well established that it was appointed as the "sole legitimate representative of the Palestinians" at an Arab summit in Rabat in 1974, to the fury of Jordan's King Hussein. In the same year Yasser Arafat, who had become chairman, was invited to address the UN General Assembly despite American and Israeli protests that he was a terrorist. The PLO split into factions, the biggest of which, Fatah, was led by Mr Arafat. The PLO received generous cheques from fellow Arabs, especially the rulers of oil-producing countries of the Gulf. These cheques financed a substantial guerrilla army. The PLO staked its claim to help by mounting terrorist attacks, most notably on airliners, to bring the attention of the world to the plight of the Palestinian refugees. It built up a base in Jordan which almost became a state within a state until King Hussein, fearing that his throne was in danger, ousted the guerrillas. They moved to Lebanon and developed a state within a state there.

Israel invades Lebanon

Israeli anger over terrorist and military attacks by the PLO from Lebanon boiled over in 1982. The hardline prime minister, Menachem Begin, and his defence minister, Ariel Sharon, wanted to defeat the PLO once and for all. Israel's 1982 attack, intended as an incursion, met little resistance and the Israelis surrounded Muslim West Beirut. After a siege, the PLO fighters were obliged to leave. Under Israeli eyes, Christian militiamen subsequently entered two Palestinian refugee camps, Sabra and Chatila, and massacred their civilian inhabitants. An Israeli inquiry later found that the government was indirectly responsible, by not having supervised the militias properly and by failing to react to reports of militiamen entering the camps. Mr Arafat moved to Tunis.

War and peace

In 1987 the Palestinians in Gaza and the West Bank launched their uprising (*intifada*), provoked by decades of ill-treatment by the Israelis, poverty, unemployment and bad living conditions. It was also a protest against the large number of Israeli settlements in the West Bank, Gaza and the Golan Heights. The *intifada* amounted to strikes, demonstrations and stone-throwing by boys. Israel's response was tough: hundreds of Palestinians were killed. (At the same time, many Palestinians suspected of working with the Israelis were killed by Palestinian extremists.) Nonetheless, a framework for peace talks was created at the Madrid conference in 1991: committees were formed for bilateral deals between Israel and its neighbours. The PLO was indirectly represented by Palestinians in a joint Jordanian-Palestinian delegation.

In 1993, after secret meetings in Norway, however, Israel and the PLO stunned the world by recognising each other and agreeing on a Declaration of Principles paving the way to a two-state solution to the dispute. In the first stage in 1994, the PLO took charge of the Gaza strip and the West Bank town of Jericho. Mr Arafat became president of the Palestinian Authority. The next stage was to be to hold elections and negotiate a "final settlement" of the status of the West Bank with an elected Palestinian administration. The limited agreement was enough to clear the way in October 1994 for Israel and Jordan to sign a peace treaty, but by early 1995 Israel had declined to withdraw its troops from the West Bank during the elections.

Enemies of peace

Hardline Palestinians, especially those in the Islamist movement Hamas and its military wing, the Brigades of Ezzeldin Qassem, opposed the PLO's step-by-step approach. A long struggle for power between the PLO and Hamas seemed to be inevitable. After Hamas extremists kidnapped an Israeli soldier in 1994 it was police of the PLO-led Palestinian authority, and not the Israelis, who detained more than 100 suspected Hamas members. The leaders of Hamas had a visceral hatred for Israel rooted, in part, in Israel's treatment of dissident Palestinians. In its 1994 report covering 1993, Amnesty International said: "At the end of the year about 10,400 remained held... Palestinians were systematically tortured or ill-treated during interrogation. Three died in custody... About 150 Palestinians were shot dead by Israeli forces." At the same time, Palestinian "freedom fighters" and "suicide bombers" killed 22 Israeli soldiers in early 1995.

Bitter rivals

The PLO, and Mr Arafat's Fatah faction, was responsible for acts of anti-Israeli terrorism in the early days. But it became increasingly non-violent, reaching the point when Mr Arafat, under powerful western pressure, publicly abjured terrorism. The dirty work was done by the Fatah Revolutionary Command led by the arch-terrorist Abu Nidal (Sabri el-Banna) and Syrian-backed hardline factions led by George Habash, Ahmed Jibril, Naif Hawatmeh and Abu Musa. With six other groups they later formed the "rejectionist front" opposed to peace between Israel and the PLO and especially to Mr Arafat. In 1994 rivalry was growing inside the PLO as well: between leaders who had spent most of their life abroad working for the organisation and those who had stayed at home and endured the Israeli occupation. Within Fatah there were those who favoured harder and softer lines with the Israelis. There was growing criticism of Mr Arafat's autocratic leadership style and his penchant for signing all PLO cheques himself.

The economy: poor and under-developed

A lack of investment inhibits economic growth in the West Bank and the densely populated but less developed Gaza strip, where refugees make up 66% of the population. The Israeli shekel and the Jordanian dinar are the main currencies. The West Bank and Gaza depend heavily on jobs in Israel. Agriculture is devoted to citrus fruits, vegetables and olives and accounts for about a third of GDP; industry accounts for only 8%. Many small businesses are low-wage subcontractors to Israeli firms. Promisingly, the private sector accounts for about 85% of GDP. Israeli statistics tell a sad story: the West Bank and Gaza strip had a GDP per head in 1991 of $1,260, compared with Jordan's $1,050 and Israel's $12,032.

A Middle East peace settlement peace should unleash the frustrated entrepreneurial talents of the Palestinians. Aid was beginning to pour in from the World Bank, the United States and the European Union. But a strong sentiment was growing in Israel to cut off the daily flow of Palestinian workers from the West Bank and Gaza strip to work in Israel. In early 1995 the flow was stopped, and then relaxed somewhat, after a terrorist incident. Israelis then began talking of closing their border to Palestinians altogether. The hope was, however, that an overall Middle East settlement would open the region to a freer flow of labour as well as goods and capital – the only way to lasting prosperity.

QATAR

Total area	11,000 sq km	Population	500,000
GDP	$7.9bn	GDP per head	$15,140
Capital	Doha	Other cities	Dukhan, Umm Said

Qatar is a sparsely populated and arid peninsula which has many more expatriate residents than the indigenous population. The expatriates are attracted by the money to be made from Qatar's oil and, more important, its natural gas.

History: a British influence

During its early history Qatar was controlled by the Khalifa family of nearby Bahrain, which was better developed. The Turks took it over in 1872 and held it until the outset of the first world war, when the British moved in. In 1915, to the great annoyance of the Bahraini ruling family, the British recognised the local sheikh, Abdullah al-Thani, as amir. Abdullah promised to do deals about Qatari territory only with Britain. For its part Britain promised to protect Qatar from outside attack. Not much changed until Britain announced its decision to withdraw most of its commitments east of Suez. In 1971 Qatar's ruler, Sheikh Ahmad bin Ali al-Thani, declared independence and assumed the title of amir. A year later he was ousted by his cousin, Sheikh Khalifa bin Hamad al-Thani. The new amir kept his old job as prime minister and ruled until June 1995 when his son, Sheikh Hamad bin Khalifa al-Thani, seized power in a bloodless coup.

Politics: autocratic but quite efficient

Qatar's earnings from oil have been spent constructively. Much of the money has gone on infrastructure projects such as roads and on schools and hospitals. The amir is the strongman. There is a 30-member advisory council, which is allowed to discuss legislation. But it is appointed by the amir. In 1994 ten of the government's 18 cabinet posts were held by members of the ruling family. Sheikh Hamad, who deposed his father in mid-1995, had effectively controlled all but the Treasury since 1992. He is acknowledged as a moderniser.

Foreign policy: independent-minded

As a peninsula linked to Saudi Arabia, Qatar comes under the wing of its bigger, richer and more populous neighbour. Ties are close. Both peoples are Wahabi Muslims, who have a puritanical code of public behaviour. Nonetheless, relations deteriorated in 1992 over a territorial dispute at al-Khofous, 130km (80 miles) south of Doha which led to armed clashes. The dispute was settled with the help of Egyptian mediation. Qatar also had a dispute with Bahrain over a number of unpopulated islands in the Gulf which led to a military confrontation in 1986. Five years later Qatar took its case to the International Court and relations went downhill again.

Annoying to some

Qatar has also irritated its neighbours by other independent-minded actions. For example, it has signed several agreements with Iran and called for its inclusion in Gulf security agreements. In 1992 it reopened its embassy in Iraq and received a delegation from the Palestine Liberation Organisation, which was then being ostracised in the Gulf over its apparent support for Iraq's invasion of Kuwait. The United States was irritated at the same time over Qatar's mysterious acquisition of 12 American Stinger missiles. As a former neo-colonial power Britain might have been expected to play an important role, but Qatar buys many of its arms from France (including a fleet of Mirage-1 and Mirage-2000 jets). Qatar was host to a delegation from Israel before it signed a peace agreement with the Palestine Liberation Organisation, and discussed the possible sale of Qatar's natural gas to Israel amid protests from hardline states such as Syria. Qatar has, however, been a steady member of the Gulf Co-operation Council.

Society: a lot of foreigners

Of the 8,000 men in the army, roughly 30% are Qataris. The rest come from 20 other countries. The population, estimated at about 500,000, probably comprises only 100,000 indigenous Qataris. By one reckoning Qataris make up only about 15% of the workforce. But about half of the indigenous population is under the age of 15, so there will eventually be a surge. Many of the foreigners come from India and Pakistan and, recently, from South-East Asia.

As Wahabi Muslims, the Qataris are teetotal, by law. In 1994 a young Briton was given 50 lashes after having been found guilty by an Islamic court of selling liquor. The Briton said he was selling a car to a police sergeant and was framed: the sergeant did not testify and no evidence was presented to the court. Qatar ignored pleas for mercy. The man's back and legs were covered in weals and bruises. He said afterwards: "My life has been scarred for ever by something which I did not do." Such actions have given Qatar a reputation as an austere and dubious place in which to live and work.

Qatar had an answer

Accordingly Sheikh Khalifa decided to make Qatar more welcoming by hosting an international tennis tournament, a golf competition and an international regatta. It was the site of the Asian qualifying round for the 1994 football World Cup and Qatar would also like to host a Formula-1 grand prix. But mid-1990s Qatar still bore no comparison to cheerful and cosmopolitan Dubai further down the coast and it remained to be seen whether this new approach would work.

The economy: long life to the North Field!

Qatar's oil reserves have enabled its people to live easily, free from material want and taxes. Petrol costs about 75 US cents a gallon, less than bottled water; housing is heavily subsidised. But oil reserves may run out by 2025. In 1994 they amounted to a modest (by Gulf standards) 3.7 billion barrels. Qatar's reserves of natural gas, on the other hand, could last for 200 years, according to some experts. There are, it is said, 227,000 billion cubic feet of proven reserves. The idea is for two huge projects in the North Field, called Qatargas and Rasgas, to start to produce results by the end of the 1990s. As camels grazed nearby, a huge natural gas terminal was being built at Ras Laffan for both projects. It was due to be finished in 1995.

Just the start

Ras Laffan was designed to show the outside world that Qatar was serious about the North Field. But much more remained to be done. Qatargas's idea was to supply Japan (its best customer) with 4m tonnes of liquefied natural gas a year starting in 1997. To do this, Qatargas would need a plant to liquefy the gas and seven super-tankers. Next would come the larger Rasgas, which has been designed to export up to 9m tonnes of liquefied natural gas. In 1994 many of the contracts for financing and production were being signed. Top commercial banks in Europe and Japan were involved. There were also signs of renewed interest in a third mega-contract, the dormant Wintershall North Field project.

Meanwhile, diversify

Qatar has sought to break away from dependence on oil and natural gas by building first a fertiliser plant followed by a steel works and a petrochemicals plant. However, declining oil production meant there was less associated gas production to serve Qatari industry and, indeed, the population. Development of the North Field became a domestic imperative. Meanwhile, the new non-oil companies took off. The Qatar Petrochemical Company (QAPCO) launched a $385m expansion scheme to produce more ethylene and low-density polyethylene. The company ran a healthy profit of $55m in 1993.

The Qatar Fertiliser Company (QAFCO) was preparing to launch a $400m expansion plan with companies from Germany and Italy. The Qatar Steel Company (QASCO) had a 1993 profit of $62m with its electric arc furnace performing, it was said, at 80% above its designed capacity. It was planning to add a $40m rolling mill. The final contractual touches were being put in 1994 to a $1.1 billion for the construction of the Ras Abu Fontas B power project. The main contractor was Italy's ABB SAE Sadelmi.

Qatar Airways was planning a rapid expansion of routes and airliners. So was the Qatar National Cement Company. Qatar Flour Mills was expanding with a $22.5m project awarded to Britain's Taylor Woodrow.

The government has approved plans to set up a stock exchange. It was to be the fifth member of the Gulf Cooperation Council to have one, leaving only the United Arab Emirates out in the cold. To the big multinationals, in banking, construction and engineering, Qatar looked in the mid-1990s like a good bet.

Down on the Qatari farm

Since Qatar is arid and flat, with much saline soil, not much is grown there. In 1991 the biggest farm product (127,000 tonnes) was of forage, followed by milk and dairy products and vegetables. There is, however, a prospect of growing more. Only 7,000 hectares are being cultivated; by one reckoning about 28,000 hectares are arable. But not many Qataris relish the idea of farming under the blazing Gulf sun. So much of the dirty work is left to imported labourers.

Total area	11,000 sq km	% agricultural area	...
Capital	Doha	Highest point metres	Dukhan
Other cities	Duhkan, Umm Said		Heights 98

The economy

GDP $bn	7.9	GDP per head $	15,140
% av. ann. growth in		GDP per head in purchasing	
real GDP 1985–93	3.2	power parity $	22,910

Origins of GDP[a]	% of total	Components of GDP[b]	% of total
Agriculture	1.0	Private consumption	31.2
Industry	44.4	Public consumption	45.2
of which:		Investment	21.0
manufacturing	14.3	Exports	39.8
Services	54.6	Imports	-37.1

Production average annual change 1985–93, %

Agriculture	...	Manufacturing	...
Industry	...	Services	...

Inflation and exchange rates

Consumer price 1993 av. ann. incr.	3.0%	Riyals per $ av. 1994	3.64
Av. ann. rate 1988–93	3.3%	Riyals per SDR av. 1994	5.27

Balance of payments, reserves, aid and debt $bn

Visible exports fob	3.1	Capital balance	...
Visible imports fob	-1.8	Overall balance	...
Trade balance	1.3	Change in reserves	0.001
Invisible inflows	0.5	Level of reserves end Dec.	0.7
Invisible outflows	...	Foreign debt	1.8
Net transfers	-0.01	as % of GDP	24.0
Current account balance	-0.5	Debt service	0.2
as % of GDP	-6.4	as % of export earnings	4.8

Principal exports 1992	$m fob	Principal imports 1992	$m cif
Petroleum	2,615	Machinery & transport	
		equipment	890
		Manufactured goods	367
		Foodstuffs & live animals	255
Total	3,406	Total	2,018

Main export destinations	% of total	Main origins of imports	% of total
Japan	63.3	Japan	19.8
South Korea	8.4	United States	10.7
Brazil	4.8	United Kingdom	10.0
Singapore	3.8	France	7.7
UAE	3.3	Italy	4.9

Government
System Monarchy with provisional constitution enacted in 1970. Executive power rests with the amir, who appoints an Advisory Council.
Main political parties None

Climate and topography
Hot desert, humid and sultry in summer. Mostly flat and barren desert covered with sand and gravel.

People and society

Population m	0.5	% under 15	30.6
Pop. per sq km	41	% over 65	1.5
% urban	79	No. men per 100 women	160
% av. ann. growth 1987–92	4.9	Human Development Index	79.5
No. households m	0.05		

Life expectancy
		Education	
Men	69 yrs	Spending as % of GDP	3.4
Women	72 yrs	Mean years of schooling	5.8
Crude birth rate	21	Adult literacy %	76
Crude death rate	4	Primary school enrolment %	104
Infant mortality rate	24	Secondary school enrolment %	83
Under-5 mortality rate	32	Tertiary education enrolment %	28

Workforce	% of total	Consumer goods ownership	
Services	69	Telephone mainlines per 1,000	...
Industry	28	Televisions per 100	44.5
Agriculture	3		
% of total population	42		

Ethnic groups	% of total	Religious groups	% of total
Arab	40	Muslim	95
Pakistani	18		
Indian	18		

Tourism		Health	
Tourist receipts $m	...	Pop. per doctor	530
		Low birthweight babies	
		% of total	6
		Daily calories % of total	
		requirement	...
		% pop. with access to safe water	89

a 1992.
b 1987.

SAUDI ARABIA

Total area	2,400,900 sq km	Population	17.4m
GDP	$121bn	GDP per head	$6,958
Capital	Riyadh	Other cities	Jeddah, Mecca, Medina

For centuries Saudi Arabia was barely on the maps of the world. It was, and is, mostly desert. Empire-builders ignored it. They dubbed one part the "Empty Quarter". Saudi Arabia is now firmly on the world map for three reasons: it has the world's biggest deposits of oil and sixth biggest deposits of natural gas; the two most holy mosques of Islam are there; and the royal regime, while being eccentric, puritanical and extravagant, has presided over a relatively long period of stable economic development. Saudi Arabia has become the world's only puritanical industrialised welfare state.

History: Where the Prophet prayed

Saudi Arabia's history is rooted in religion and the rise of one family, the al-Saud. King Fahd is accorded the title of "Custodian of the Two Holy Mosques", at Mecca and Medina. It is the best credential to protect him and his family against Islamic extremists and other potential rivals. Mecca is the holiest city of the Islamic world and the spiritual heart of the city is the Haram mosque, to which all Muslims around the world direct their prayers. It is the biggest mosque in the world. There is a great esplanade at the centre of which is the Ka'aba. This is an empty stone structure with a flat roof, covered by a great silk drape, which is changed annually. In its eastern external corner is a black stone set in a silver collar, which Muslims on their pilgrimage attempt to kiss. The Ka'aba existed long before Islam was revealed to the Prophet Muhammad in the early part of the 7th century. It is associated in Islamic tradition with Abraham. Before the revelation of Islam, the Ka'aba was in the hands of the Quraysh tribe, who revered it and, in 608AD, refurbished it. Islam took it over. The Ka'aba was subsequently rebuilt by the Prophet Ibrahim and his son, Ismail.

The birth of Islam

The Prophet Muhammad, who was opposed to the decadence of his society, frequently meditated in the Cave of Hira, near the summit of the Mountain of Light, close to Mecca. At the age of 40 he said he had received his first revelation from the Angel Jibril. This revelation, which continued for 23 years, became known as the Koran. Having suffered persecution for his sermons in Mecca, the Prophet made his migration from Mecca to Medina with his followers in 622AD and set up a mosque and the simple chambers where he lived with his wives. Seven years later he and his growing number of followers arrived in Mecca and took it over. Since then Islam has spread. By 1994, according to one reckoning, there were about 1 billion Muslims. As increasing numbers came to Mecca on pilgrimage (some 2.5m a year nowadays), the keepers of the mosque expanded it so that it can now handle 730,000 worshippers at any one time. The Prophet's tomb is in Medina.

The rise of the al-Saud family

While much of the Middle East fell under Ottoman and subsequently European control, the hinterland remained under the rule of Arab dynasties. What is now central Saudi Arabia, known as the Najd, was ruled by Saud Ibn Muhammad, founder of the al-Saud dynasty, in the early part of the 18th century. He proselytised with the assistance of a religious scholar and preacher, Muhammad bin Abdel Wahab, who sought refuge with him in 1744. This charismatic scholar called for a return to the orthodox practices of early Islam. His teachings spread, and the Wahabi sect took shape. Gradually the al-Saud family's power spread: to the Empty Quarter, the Eastern Province, Mecca and Medina, and the Hejaz. Finally the Ottomans woke up to what was happening and in 1814 authorised the Egyptian army (then under Ottoman control) to recapture the holy cities. This they did. They also booted the al-Saud family out of the Najd. The rival al-Rashid family took its place. The al-Saud family went into exile in Kuwait in 1891. But in 1902 the legendary Abdulaziz Ibn Saud recaptured Riyadh from the al-Rashids and installed his family in power. He declared himself sultan of the Najd in 1926 and king of the Hejaz, including Mecca and Medina (ousting its Hashemite rulers), in 1927. Finally, on September 23rd 1932, he became king of a new country with an unusual family-linked name: Saudi Arabia. He signed a treaty of protection with Britain in 1915 and one for independence in 1927.

Stability with change

So far, the Saudi dynasty has avoided open rifts. Abdulaziz Ibn Saud was succeeded on his death in 1953 by one of his 34 surviving sons from his many wives: Saud. Many other sons took top jobs. The new king, who proved himself to be incompetent, formed a council of ministers that was mainly but not exclusively made up of men with the patronymic: "bin Abdulaziz" (son of Abdulaziz). It was less autocratic than Abdulaziz's own one-man rule. Saud was deposed in 1964 by his half-brother, Faisal, who led the country capably through a period of international turmoil. Faisal was assassinated in 1975 and succeeded by his half-brother, Khaled, who died of a heart attack in 1982. Yet another half-brother, Fahd, took over. All of the monarchs were conservative, cautious men who saw the opportunity of consolidating the position of their family through the judicious expenditure of the kingdom's vast oil revenues.

There was widespread talk of fabulously rich Saudi princes getting big percentages of contracts with foreign companies in return for piloting them through to final approval. Nonetheless, much of the money was turned into bricks and mortar for buildings that were put to good use. (Prince Al-Waleed Bin Tallaal, for example, is the biggest private shareholder in Citicorp, America's biggest bank, and a major investor in Euro Disney, Saks Fifth Avenue and the American Fairmont hotel chain.) Saudi Arabia established a competent welfare state for its citizens with free healthcare and education.

Fahd, described by some westerners as a sort of Saudi Ronald Reagan, was said to be an easy-going man in frail health who, when relaxing, enjoyed cracking jokes. His named successor, Crown Prince Abdullah, commander of the national guard, was due to succeed him, provided that he won support from Abdulaziz's sons and grandsons meeting in a family conclave. If not, the next king might be Prince Sultan, the defence minister. But these elderly men would sooner rather than later be succeeded by the al-Saud family's next generation. One of the favourites was King Fahd's son, Prince Muhammad. He is governor of the sensitive Eastern Province with its large Shia Muslim population, where the Wahabis are in a minority. The political and economic power of the king is so great and the stakes so high that a succession struggle, and a period of instability, could not be ruled out.

Politics: democracy, did you say?

In the aftermath of the 1990–91 Gulf war to remove Iraqi occupation troops from neighbouring Kuwait, the international spotlight was turned on the autocratic way Kuwait had been governed by its ruling family, and also on Saudi Arabia, the operational base for the American-led coalition forces. So in 1992 King Fahd published a basic law setting up a consultative council (majlis al-shoura) and regional councils. However, political parties are banned and the 60-man consultative council is not elected. The king himself must approve if the council is to question cabinet ministers and have access to state documents. The council can vote on motions to be put before the king but neither he nor the cabinet need take any notice of them if they disagree with the conclusions. It may not be much but, in a fairly closed society, it is at least a start. Other political pressures exist: before independence, Mecca, Medina and Jiddah had much more importance than they have now, with the country ruled by a family from the centre. Most people are, however, so well off that this may not matter.

The royal family tries to rule by consensus and to take note of changing attitudes in the armed forces, the national guard, the religious establishment and the business world. Prince Sultan and Crown Prince Abdullah control the armed forces and national guard fairly well. Western-educated Saudi businessmen are in many cases much more liberal than the ruling family, but do not complain much because they have (until recently) been making pots of money. The royal family has, by its rules on public behaviour and its guardianship of the holy places, avoided being vulnerable to criticism from fundamentalists. Nonetheless, the recently formed Committee for the Defence of Legal Rights, an Islamist grouping, has called for the release of preachers imprisoned by the government for opposing pro-western policies. The commission has been closed. In September 1993 the authorities acknowledged the arrest of 110 men with ties to unidentified "foreign interests" who were plotting to "spread sedition".

Foreign policy: a bitter pill

Iraq's occupation of Kuwait, and apparent intention of occupying the oil-producing Saudi Eastern Province next door, taught the al-Saud family a lesson. Yemen and Jordan, two client states, and the Palestine Liberation Organisation, recipient of Saudi millions, appeared to support the invasion and made ambiguous statements about it. Other Arab states took the Kuwaiti and Saudi side, but only after a tough bout of cheque-book diplomacy. The only reliable friends were the United States, Britain and France. And they were helpful only because of their need to protect Kuwaiti and Saudi oil reserves. There was a bill to pay to them, too, in huge contracts for armaments, telecommunications and airliners. Saudi Arabia is the leading member of the Gulf Co-operation Council (GCC), which also includes Kuwait,

Bahrain, Qatar, the United Arab Emirates and Oman. Sporadic attempts to create a joint armed force before the Gulf war had failed. So the GCC was not much help. With holier-than-thou Iran glowering at them across the Gulf, the Saudis feel isolated and annoyed.

One success

Nonetheless, they have tried to have an impact in the Arab world as a peacemaker and have scored one bull's-eye: by hosting an extraordinary session of the Lebanese parliament in the Saudi city of Taif, they helped to bring an end to the Lebanese civil war. The Saudis have always been worried about neighbouring Yemen, with its large population and its many immigrant workers based in Saudi Arabia. After Yemen appeared to support Iraq's occupation of Kuwait, the Saudis withdrew the work permits of thousands of mostly unskilled workers. It was particularly worrying when Yemen had a free and fair general election in 1990, setting an example (temporarily) to the Arab world. When in 1994 southern Yemenis launched a separatist rebellion, the Saudis were said by some diplomats to have backed them. But the rebellion collapsed. Subsequently, border troubles, possibly promoted by the Saudis, were settled in 1995 on terms thought to be favourable to Saudi Arabia.

Society: eccentric

While in the western world progress is regularly made towards equality for women, Saudi Arabia remains in the middle ages. Women may not wear short-sleeved clothes or western-style skirts. They may not drive cars. They may enter supermarkets unaccompanied, but only on women-only days. Alcohol is banned. Thieves have a hand chopped off. Drug-dealers are beheaded. Satellite dishes capable of picking up corrupting western films and subversive news programmes are banned.

The economy: trouble looms

The al-Saud family's consistent policy since 1962 has been to diversify out of oil, trade and services into industry so that, a hundred years hence, when when the oil runs out, they will have something else to keep them going. Saudi businessmen have not been convinced. So the family has done the job itself through the state. The development plan for the five years to 1995 called for spending on education, health, roads, telephones, waterworks, power supply and farming, and for the construction of factories. There was no mention of privatisation. Saudi Arabia is dirigiste. Its proven recoverable oil reserves in 1993 were estimated at 257,000m barrels, equal to just over a quarter of the world's total known reserves. Most of the oil is pumped by Saudi Aramco, which is responsible for 99% of crude oil production and all natural gas liquids. Production grew rapidly, except in the period of the Arab oil embargo. In 1992 production of crude oil was put at 8.2m barrels a day. Some is taken to customers from Gulf terminals; the rest goes by pipeline across the country to the Red Sea terminal at Yanbu. Proven gas reserves in 1993 amounted to 183 trillion cubic feet. These were the fifth largest in the world after the ex-Soviet Union, Iran, Qatar and the United Arab Emirates.

Huge investments have been made in refineries and plants to make methane, ethane, sulphur, bulk chemicals, plastics, fertiliser and other products based on oil and gas, adding value to both. Investments have also been made at Jubail in the east and at Yanbu in manufacturing. Such staggering riches have made Saudi Arabia prosper. But the economy could have been managed better. Much of the money has been spent and, incredibly, Saudi Arabia is sinking into debt. Thanks to oil and gas, it does have an in-built trade surplus. But it has a current-account deficit which it has partly been covering by running down its foreign exchange reserves, from a respectable $22.6 billion in 1987 to a humble $6.5 billion in June 1994. Saudi Arabia also has a worrying budget deficit.

Promises, promises

The government says it wants to balance the budget. But the deficit was 8.7% of GDP in 1992 and 9.2% in 1993; it was projected at 7.8% in 1994 and 7% in 1995. This little matter could be tidied up in a few months if the government imposed a tax. It said in 1994 that it was cutting spending by 19%. But the only likely cut was one on the high subsidy for home-grown wheat, which would fall far short of the target. According to the sixth development plan, ending in 2000, much more emphasis is to be laid on the private sector, on its own and in joint projects with the government as well as on possible privatisation. However, there was not much sign of impending action. Saudi Arabia is so rich that it will survive even if it does nothing. But the government has already had to cancel some arms purchases and delay some international payments. At the same time, it has announced massive new arms and telecommunications purchases. If it continues to neglect the country's finances, the currency may have to be devalued.

Total area	2,400,900 sq km	% agricultural area	1
Capital	Riyadh	Highest point metres	3,133
Other cities	Jeddah, Mecca, Medina		

The economy

GDP $bn	121.0	GDP per head $	6,958
% av. ann. growth in		GDP per head in purchasing	
real GDP 1985–93	4.1	power parity $	...

Origins of GDP[a]	% of total	Components of GDP[b]	% of total
Agriculture	7.3	Private consumption	38.3
Industry	45.5	Public consumption	36.6
of which:		Investment	24.4
manufacturing	8.1	Exports	39.5
Services	44.2	Imports	-38.9

Production average annual change 1985–93, %

Agriculture	14.0	Manufacturing	8.1
Industry	-2.9	Services	-0.2

Inflation and exchange rates

Consumer price 1993 av. ann. incr.	1.0%	Riyals per $ av. 1994	3.75
Av. ann. rate 1988–93	1.8%	Riyals per SDR av. 1994	5.42

Balance of payments, reserves, aid and debt

			$bn
Visible exports fob	44.9	Capital balance	14.2
Visible imports fob	-25.9	Overall balance	1.5
Trade balance	19.0	Change in reserves	1.5
Invisible inflows	9.7	Level of reserves end Dec.	7.7
Invisible outflows	-26.3	Foreign debt	19.5
Net transfers	-16.7	as % of GDP	16.0
Current account balance	-14.2	Debt service	2.4
as % of GDP	-11.8	as % of export earnings	4.5

Principal exports[c]	$bn fob	Principal imports[c]	$bn cif
Crude oil &		Transport equipment	7.0
refined petroleum	43.7	Consumer goods	5.2
Petrochemicals & plastics	2.4	Machinery	4.6
		Foodstuffs	3.6
		Building materials	3.3
Total	48.2	Total	29.1

Main export destinations	% of total	Main origins of imports	% of total
Japan	17.1	United States	20.6
United States	16.2	Japan	12.7
South Korea	8.2	United Kingdom	8.5
Singapore	5.7	Germany	7.2
France	5.2	Italy	6.3
United Kingdom	3.7	France	4.3

Government
System Absolute monarchy ruled by the king who also appoints a Council of Ministers.
Main political parties None

Climate and topography
Very dry with great extremes of temperature. Mostly uninhabited desert.

People and society

Population m	17.4	% under 15	42.0
Pop. per sq km	8	% over 65	2.7
% urban	78	No. men per 100 women	124
% av. ann. growth 1987–92	3	Human Development Index	74.2
No. households m	…		

Life expectancy		Education	
Men	70 yrs	Spending as % of GDP	6.2
Women	73 yrs	Mean years of schooling	3.9
Crude birth rate	35	Adult literacy %	64.1
Crude death rate	4	Primary school enrolment %	77
Infant mortality rate	28	Secondary school enrolment %	46
Under-5 mortality rate	38	Tertiary education enrolment %	13

Workforce	% of total	Consumer goods ownership	
Services	37	Telephone mainlines per 1,000	78
Industry	14	Televisions per 100	26.9
Agriculture	48		
% of total population	29		

Ethnic groups	% of total	Religious groups	% of total
Arab	90	Muslim	100
Afro-Asian	10		

Tourism		Health	
Tourist receipts $m	1,000	Pop. per doctor	700
		Low birthweight babies % of total	7
		Daily calories % of total requirement	120
		% pop. with access to safe water	93

a 1989.
b 1992.
c 1991.

SYRIA

Total area	185,180 sq km	Population	13.3m
GDP	$16.2bn	GDP per head	$1,210
Capital	Damascus	Other cities	Aleppo, Homs

As this book was being written, Syria and Israel were the keys to an overall peace settlement in the Middle East. The leaders of both countries said they wanted peace. But, true to a tradition that goes back to the third millennium, they were bargainers to their finger-tips.

History: oldest capital?

Syria's origins are in the depths of history. The Canaanites and the Phoenicians arrived in what is now Syria in the third millennium, the Hebrews and the Arameans in the second and Damascus, founded in about 2000BC, lays claim to being the world's oldest capital. The Romans trampled over it in the first century AD, followed by Egyptians, Assyrians, Hittites and Persians. Present-day Syria attained the peak of its power when, after the death of the Prophet Muhammad in 632AD, the founders of the Arab-Islamic empire, the Omayyads (661–750), arrived. They ruled over "Greater Syria": present-day Syria, Israel, Lebanon and Jordan. The Omayyads eventually created an empire stretching from Spain, North Africa and the Gulf to India. They had their seat in Damascus. To the Damascenes' disgust, however, the Omayyads' successors, the Abbasids, moved to Iraq. After the Seljuk Turks made a hash of running the area in 1075 (when they seized Damascus), it was the turn of the Crusaders, who arrived in 1098. Their temporary dominance was ended in 1291 thanks to opposition from the Muslim Saladin and, after him, the Mameluks of Egypt. Greater Syria fell under the power of the Ottoman Empire in 1516, where it remained until the first world war.

The carve-up

After the first world war, the influence of the Turks, who sided with the Germans, was ended. Through the Sykes-Picot treaty of 1916, Britain and France shared out spheres of influence in the old Ottoman empire. Syria (including Lebanon) was to be in the French sphere; Iraq and Palestine would be British. This was confirmed in 1920 by the San Remo agreement. In the same year, however, a Syrian Congress chose Prince Faisal, son of King Hussein of the Hejaz (part of present-day Saudi Arabia) as king. Faisal had received promises by the wartime allies that the peoples of the Near East, in return for help in the war against the

Ottoman empire, would be allowed to be free from outside rule. Instead, Faisal was expelled from Syria by France (he later became, with the help of the British, king of Iraq). Also the French split Syria in two: Syria, with its capital in Damascus, and Lebanon, with its capital at Beirut. For the next 16 years the French ruled Syria, building roads and organising government institutions while facing growing discontent from a people who wanted them to go. Anti-French demonstrations erupted. In 1936 France's Popular Front government signed a treaty giving independence in principle to Syria; it would come into force in three years, when the Damascus government would be ready. But in 1938 the French government decided not to ratify it. During the second world war, British, Commonwealth and Free French troops ousted pro-Vichy forces from Syria in 1941. General Catroux, on behalf of the Free French, proclaimed Syria's independence. Somewhat unwillingly the Free French agreed to hold an election in 1943, after which a nationalist, Shukri al-Kuwatli, was elected as head of government. Nonetheless, Syria remained in the French sphere. In 1945 anti-French demonstrations took place and the British intervened to restore order, and to ease the speedy departure of the French. By 1946 the British had gone as well.

What freedom?

Independence brought years of instability marked by frequent military coups. France continued to provide aid but was widely seen to be meddling. There was no convincing national leader. In March 1949 a colonel overthrew the Kuwatli government. Another colonel ousted him in August, and was removed in November by Colonel Adib Shishakli (who subsequently removed his co-conspirators in a mini-coup in 1951). An election in 1953 was boycotted by the established parties and was won by Shishakli's party. Shishakli ruled in association with conservative civilian politicians until he was forced to flee to France in 1954. The following year an election was held and Kuwatli, the civilian leader, became president. Syrians argued over what course in the Middle East their country should follow. Some favoured closer relations with Egypt, led at the time by the pan-Arab nationalist strongman, Gamal Abdel Nasser. Others dreamed of a Syrian-led alliance of many Arab states.

A short-lived marriage

The Nasserites won, and in 1957 the national assembly voted to set up the United Arab Republic with Egypt. It lasted only until 1961 when army officers, unhappy at the way Egypt was dominating it, seized power and withdrew from it. They lasted until 1963 when armed forces officers supporting the Baath Socialist Party took power. The party believed in socialism and a pan-Arab union and promptly nationalised the banks, confirming its socialism. But after a power struggle, nationalist opponents of pan-Arabism emerged the victors. Among the military leaders in the Baath Party were increasing numbers of Alawites, members of a schismatic Muslim sect comprising 11% of the population. Under General Salah Jadid and his civilian supporters, the government was committed to a collectivist, state-run economy and a "people's war of liberation" against Israel. Salah Jadid, who was assistant secretary-general of the Baath Party, was ousted in 1970 by the defence minister, General Hafez Assad, who favoured an accommodation with the private sector, more political participation for non-Baathists, an end to Syria's isolation and a strengthening of the army. The socialist ideologues were jailed. Under the amended constitution, Mr Assad became president, commander-in-chief and leader of the Baath Party. There is a tame People's Assembly, for which there were elections in 1990 and 1994. Unlike neighbouring Jordan there is no serious parliamentary opposition. Mr Assad was "elected" as president in 1971 and "re-elected" in 1978, 1985 and 1991.

Wars with Israel

In the 1967 six-day war with the Arabs, Israel seized the Sinai desert from Egypt, the West Bank from Jordan and, after a literally uphill battle, the Golan Heights above Lake Tiberias from Syria. It also seized the town of Kuneitra, about 65km (40 miles) from Damascus. In the 1973 Yom Kippur war, Israel suffered some setbacks at the hands of Anwar Sadat's Egyptians but did well against the Syrians. Although the Syrian army had the advantage of fighting a surprised enemy and advancing downhill, a much smaller Israeli force, aided by warplanes, fought back well. It not only stopped the advance but also counter-attacked. By the end of the war Israel controlled more Syrian territory and threatened Damascus. In the following year, after "shuttle diplomacy" by the American secretary of state, Henry Kissinger, the two sides agreed on a "disengagement of forces". Mr Assad promised to prevent Palestinian guerrillas from using Syrian territory to attack Israel. He kept his word. But an angry and humiliated Syria has remained the most difficult of Israel's neighbours. Mr Assad condemned the 1978 Camp David peace agreement between Israel and Egypt, demanding a full Israeli withdrawal behind the pre-

1967 border. He was even angrier when, in 1982, Israel formally annexed the Golan Heights. Determined never again to be bested by Israeli military power, Syria became a close ally of the Soviet Union and purchaser of the latest Soviet Mig aircraft, missiles, radar and warships. In 1980 there were more than 4,000 Soviet military advisers in the country, and a big bill to pay. The Syrian armed forces, though smaller and less effective than Israel's, became a serious cause for concern in Israel.

Syria's dreams of empire

Perhaps harking back to the days of "Greater Syria", Mr Assad has always had his beady eye on Lebanon, the Palestinians and Iraq. He drew Lebanon into Syria's area of influence by gradually inserting Syrian military units in the country as peacemakers and peacekeepers. The warring Lebanese, more interested in killing each other, did little about it. In fact Syria's intervention helped to end the fighting. Syria's influence became so strong, following the signature of "co-operation" agreements by the two countries in 1991, that the Lebanese prime minister checked with Syria before taking any important decision. Some 40,000 Syrian troops were said to be based in Lebanon, many of them in the Bekaa valley.

Whose Palestinians?

President Assad would also have liked to exercise the same control over the Palestinians but the chairman of the Palestine Liberation Organisation (PLO), Yasser Arafat, outwitted him. The two men became bitter enemies. Mr Assad allowed hardline dissident Palestinian factions, opposed to Mr Arafat, to base themselves in Damascus. Among them were the Popular Front for the Liberation of Palestine and the followers of the arch-terrorist Abu Nidal. Mr Assad helped to form a rival PLO under the dissident Abu Musa, but the venture failed. Although the dissidents remained in Damascus, and rejected the peace pact between Israel and the PLO, international terrorism waned. By 1994 it seemed to be over. (Syria's air force intelligence service was blamed for some pro-Palestinian terrorism in 1986; worryingly, the general in charge of it at the time was in 1994 named as air force commander.)

Whose Baath Party?

The Baath parties in Syria and Iraq are rivals. Presidents Assad and Hussein are bitter enemies. Their countries are rivals for regional power. In 1982 Mr Assad switched off the pipeline which carried Iraqi oil to a Lebanese terminal on the Mediterranean via Syria, obliging Iraq to build a longer pipeline via Turkey. Mr Assad formed a strategic relationship with Iran and helped the Iranians in their 1980–88 war with Iraq. In return, Syria obtained Iranian oil at subsidised prices. During the war to evict Iraq from its occupation of Kuwait, Syria sent its troops to join the American-led anti-Iraqi coalition. Mr Assad gained some international respectability by that gesture. He may have hoped that if Mr Hussein lost power in Baghdad, Syria's influence could spread there, as it had in Lebanon.

Only one friend

The collapse of the Soviet Union left Syria with only one, somewhat dubious, ally: Iran. Mr Assad knew he could obtain no more arms from Moscow on credit (he had an unpaid bill reckoned at between $10 billion and $12 billion). The Russians told him he could never expect to achieve "strategic parity" with Israel (which had been his dream) and that he must make do with the ability for "sufficient self-defence". He knew that Syria was low on Russia's list of priorities and that his military arsenal was wearing out. He was also painfully aware that, in dealing with Israel, he had only one serious go-between: the United States. By early 1995, while the PLO and Jordan had made their peace with Israel and were trying to implement it, Mr Assad and his cohort, Lebanon, were out in the cold. The pressures were growing on him, and on Israel, to reach an agreement before the 1996 American and Israeli election campaigns. The idea was for Israel to hand over, in stages, the Golan Heights to Syria and its security zone in south Lebanon to Lebanon. In return, Syria and Lebanon would open full diplomatic and trade relations with Israel, bringing peace at last to the Near East.

Politics: the price of stability

By 1994 Mr Assad almost looked like a moderate. There was little or no sign of Damascus-based international terrorism. He was host to frequent visits from American officials trying to start a negotiation between Syria and Israel. It was recognised that Mr Assad had given Syria and Lebanon a taste of stability. There was a tendency to forget that the price has been killings, torture, arbitrary detention of political prisoners and the absence of due process of law. In 1982, for example, Mr Assad put down a revolt in Hama with great ferocity: after a prolonged artillery barrage, the town was assaulted by infantry and tanks; hundreds are said to have been killed. The launching of trials before the feared Supreme State Security Court in 1992 was an attempt to make Syria look better in the eyes of the outside world. Political detainees with suspected communist connections were given harsh jail sentences. Amnesty International said many defendants had no defence lawyer and were not allowed to appeal. But more than 4,000 political prisoners were released between December 1991 and December 1992, and more were released in 1993, the New York-based Human Rights Watch reported. Nonetheless, the civil-rights violations would not be forgotten. One man had been held without trial since 1969. Ex-general Salah Jadid, the former Baath leader, died after 23 years in detention.

How stable will Syria be after Mr Assad goes? Syria could return to the bad old days. The Sunnis might want to oust the Alawites from power. Mr Assad was grooming his son Bashir to succeed him after an elder son, Basil, was killed in a car accident. But Bashir, a surgeon by training, may not survive Syria's ruthless power politics.

The economy: opening up

One of the keys to President Assad's survival was his partial liberalisation of the economy, giving the merchants of Damascus a relatively free hand to make money. Prudent economic management helped. Inflation in 1992 and 1993 was about 18%; GDP grew by 9.6% in 1992 and 5% in 1993. As a front-line state, Syria spent much of its government revenues on arms purchases. However, part of the money came in the form of gifts from Gulf states. For many years, agriculture (wheat, barley and cotton) was the mainstay of the economy. But the discoveries of oilfields since 1984 (Syria had proven reserves of 1.73 billion barrels in 1994) and the exploitation of big natural gas resources (about 225 billion cubic metres) have set the economy on the road to stronger and steadier growth. Petroleum and petroleum products account for nearly two-thirds of Syria's exports. Mining of phospates is growing. But manufacturing has been marked by under-utilised capacity owing to a shortage of foreign exchange. Syria's foreign debt in 1994 was put at $16 billion. There were plans for the "forgiveness" of part of it by Russia and the European Union, as a "peace dividend". Syria was running a trade and current-account deficit in the 1990s. More free-market reforms were needed, including a unified exchange rate, an opening up of the antiquated state-run banking system and the establishment of a stockmarket.

Total area	185,180 sq km	% agricultural area	33
Capital	Damascus	Highest point metres	Mt Hermon
Other cities	Aleppo, Homs,		2,814
	Latakia	Main rivers	Euphrates, Orontes

The economy

GDP $bn	16.2	GDP per head $	1,210
% av. ann. growth in		GDP per head in purchasing	
real GDP 1985–93	4.2	power parity $	...

Origins of GDP	% of total	Components of GDP	% of total
Agriculture	30.0	Private consumption	...
Industry	23.0	Public consumption	...
of which:		Investment	84.8
manufacturing	...	Exports	28.5
Services	48.0	Imports	28.3

Production average annual change 1985–93, %

Agriculture	-0.3	Manufacturing	...
Industry	7.6	Services	0.3

Inflation and exchange rates

Consumer price 1993 av. ann. incr.	18.0%	Pounds per $ av. 1994	11.23
Av. ann. rate 1988–93	11.9%	Pounds per SDR av. 1994	16.24

Balance of payments, reserves, aid and debt

			$bn
Visible exports fob	3.2	Capital balance	0.6
Visible imports fob	3.4	Overall balance	0.1
Trade balance	-0.2	Change in reserves	0.2
Invisible inflows	1.5	Level of reserves end Dec.	2.6
Invisible outflows	-2.6	Foreign debt	19.9
Net transfers	0.9	as % of GDP	122.8
Current account balance	-0.3	Debt service	1.3
as % of GDP	-2.0	as % of export earnings	5.3

Principal exports*	$m fob	Principal imports*	$m cif
Crude petroleum	1,850.6	Machinery	622.7
Vegetables & fruit	234.6	Metals & manufactures	514.6
Textiles	233.1	Transport equipment	459.1
Cotton	181.6	Resins	264.7
		Textiles	262.1
Total	3,093.1	Total	3,490.3

Main export destinations	% of total	Main origins of imports	% of total
Italy	29.1	Germany	12.9
France	16.4	Italy	11.5
Germany	8.5	Turkey	8.8
Ex-Soviet Union	1.8	France	8.7

Government

System Republic. Legislative unicameral People's Council is elected for a 4-year term. Executive power vested in president and Council of Ministers.
Main political parties Baath Party, Arab Socialist Unionist Party, Syrian Arab Socialist Unity Party, Arab Socialist Party

Climate and topography

Hot, dry and sunny summers, with mild, rainy winters along coast. Narrow coastal plain, desert plateau and mountains in the west.

People and society

Population m	13.3	% under 15	49.2
Pop. per sq km	72	% over 65	4.4
% urban	51	No. men per 100 women	104
% av. ann. growth 1987–92	3.4	Human Development Index	72.7
No. households m	1.4		

Life expectancy		Education	
Men	65 yrs	Spending as % of GDP	...
Women	69 yrs	Mean years of schooling	4.2
Crude birth rate	42	Adult literacy %	66.6
Crude death rate	6	Primary school enrolment %	109
Infant mortality rate	36	Secondary school enrolment %	21
Under-5 mortality rate	50	Tertiary education enrolment %	19

Workforce	% of total	Consumer goods ownership	
Services	36	Telephone mainlines per 1,000	41
Industry	32	Televisions per 100	6
Agriculture	32		
% of total population	28		

Ethnic groups	% of total	Religious groups	% of total
Arab	90	Sunni Muslim	74
Kurd, Armenian & other	10	Alawite, Druze and other Muslim	16

Tourism		Health	
Tourist receipts $m	600	Pop. per doctor	1,160
		Low birthweight babies	
		% of total	11
		Daily calories % of total	
		requirement	126
		% pop. with access to safe water	73

a 1992.

TUNISIA

Total area	163,610 sq km	Population	8.4m
GDP	$15.3bn	GDP per head	$1,780
Capital	Tunis	Other cities	Sfax, Bizerte

Tunisia is relatively well-developed and maintains a strong French influence. It is very close to Europe, being only about 160km (100 miles) from Sicily. But it is still poor and suffers from high unemployment. It has been dominated since the end of the second world war by French colonial rulers and two strongmen.

History: unwanted visitors

The Carthaginian empire based in what is now Tunisia reached the height of its power in the 4th century BC, but was destroyed by the Romans in the three Punic Wars (264–241, 218–201 and 149–146). Carthage was rebuilt and prospered under Augustus but was subsequently taken over by the Vandals and later became part of the Byzantine empire. There followed a stream of Arab and Berber rulers, Italians, Normans and Spaniards until the beys of Tunis provided stable government in the 18th century. Financial collapse led to intervention by France, Britain and Italy in 1869; French forces seized control in 1881, setting up a protectorate two years later. By the 1920s Tunisian nationalists had formed the Destour (Constitution) party and later the Neo-Destour party to call for independence. This came, after a period of autonomy, in 1956. All 98 seats in the Constituent Assembly were won in the election of that year by the Neo-Destour. Its leader, Habib Bourguiba, became prime minister and, after the bey of Tunis was deposed in 1957, president. Bourguiba jailed or exiled his enemies, notably Salah ben Youssef. Ambitious but non-rebellious politicians were frequently hired and fired before they could establish their own power base. Regularly re-elected without opposition, Bourguiba remained as president until 1987 when, senile, he was removed from office in a peaceful coup.

No give and take

The only real opposition that was allowed to exist came from the General Union of Tunisian Workers (UGTT) under Habib Achour, who became a thorn in Bourguiba's side for many years. There were ripples of social unrest but when a cabinet minister suggested this was due to unemployment and the fast growth of the population, Bourguiba fired him. Tunisia's inefficient socialist economy (all foreign-owned land had been appropriated) became a breeding ground for fundamentalists who formed the relatively moderate Islamic Tendency Movement. Bourguiba misguidedly regarded it as a deadly enemy and cracked down. Many moderates were arrested, and thus radicalised. The movement's leader, Rachid Ghannouchi, was arrested in 1987. Bourguiba accused the Islamists of working in collusion with Iran to overthrow the government. The Islamists denied it, and accused the police of torture. Only licensed parties could contest elections; their vote had to reach 5% nationwide before they were eligible for a single parliamentary seat. Thus the Destour Socialist Party (as it was renamed) created a one-party state. Bourguiba became "president-for-life". Opposition parties usually boycotted elections on the ground that they were loaded in favour of the ruling party.

Politics: unfulfilled hopes

Bourguiba appointed General Zine al-Abidine Ben Ali as prime minister in the belief that this former intelligence chief was trustworthy. He was wrong: Mr Ben Ali ousted the president in 1987 after seven doctors had duly signed a statement that he was too sick to govern. Bourguiba spent his declining years outside Tunis in relative luxury in a house that was described as a "gilded cage". Many Tunisians hoped that Mr Ben Ali would provide a breath of fresh air, and he claimed to be more democratic than Bourguiba. The post of president-for-life was abolished; the president was to be elected every five years for only two terms; and no presidential candidate could be more than 70 years old. The streets named after Bourguiba were renamed, and the statues of the great man were quietly taken down. President Ben Ali endorsed multi-party democracy. The repressive press law was relaxed. Some, though not all, political prisoners were released. And yet Mr Ben Ali seemed to be walking in Bourguiba's footsteps. The Destour Socialist Party changed its name to the Democratic Constitutional Rally but, in the 1989 election, the "new" party won every seat in parliament and General Ben Ali was elected unopposed.

What democracy?

Six parties were recognised by the government: the centre-left Democratic Socialists' Movement; the Pan-Arab, centre-left Popular Unity Party; the Progressive Socialist Assembly; the Social Progress Party; the Unionist Democratic Union; and the Renovation Movement (formerly the Communist

Party). None had any clout. The opposition party which mattered, the Islamic Tendency Movement, renamed as the Renewal Party, was not officially recognised and could not take part in elections. The president said he opposed purely religious parties and pressed the Renewal leaders to clarify their position on the status of women. In 1990 an arms cache was discovered and Renewal followers were blamed for a supposed plot against the state. Another plot was discovered a year later and 300 people were arrested. The government offered a special deal to the official opposition in the 1990 local elections: the winning party was to get only 50% of the seats and the rest were to be distributed equitably between the other parties. The opposition rejected this offer, claiming the election would be rigged, and did not take part. The president's apparent efforts to achieve consensus failed but he could blame the opposition for not seizing an opportunity.

It's me again

The presidential election of 1994 was won by General Ben Ali with 99.91% of the vote. He was the only candidate, two rivals having been unable to garner the support of the 30 MPs or mayors needed to qualify (all MPs and mayors were members of the ruling party). The general was supported by the six official opposition parties and the formerly opposition trade union. In the parliamentary election the ruling party won 97.7% of the vote and all 144 seats allocated on a first-past-the-post system. The six opposition parties, which gained 2.2% of the vote, were under a special deal given 19 seats. The Renewal Party was banned and most of its leaders were in jail or in exile. President Ben Ali said Tunisia had achieved multi-party democracy.

Many observers said the election was reasonably fair though some questioned the polling-station procedures. The opposition was given time on radio and television and space on election billboards to present its ideas; its expenses were subsidised by the government. On the other hand, a lawyer who dared to put his name forward as a presidential candidate and call for greater political freedom was detained for ten weeks. Another potential presidential candidate was arrested after he called for more political freedom and legalisation of the Renewal Party.

The government lashed out at criticism in the foreign press. It was deeply unhappy when the American State Department reported in 1993 on "widespread human-rights abuses including torture" in Tunisia. On the other hand, President Ben Ali has given Tunisia a period of stability (a sharp contrast to neighbouring Algeria and Libya) in which he has neutered the Islamists and achieved economic growth.

Foreign policy: moderation above all

Under Presidents Bourguiba and Ben Ali, Tunisia has played a moderate, conciliatory role in the Arab-Israeli dispute, and has often landed in trouble with radical Arab leaders for doing so. It provided a home for the Palestine Liberation Organisation (which on at least one occasion was raided by Israeli commandos). This convenient base served as an invaluable point of contact between the PLO and Israel, its Arab neighbours, the United States and West European governments. In 1994 President Ben Ali took over the one-year presidency of the Organisation of African Unity from Egypt's President Hosni Mubarak. Tunisia is also an enthusiastic member of the Arab Maghreb Union.

The economy: free-market reforms

Under Bourguiba, Tunisia adopted socialist economic policies. President Ben Ali has been changing them. Starting in 1989 the government began the process of trade liberalisation, strengthening the private sector, restructuring state enterprises and introducing tax reforms. By 1994 it had opened an interbank foreign exchange market, it was reforming the sensitive employment law, the stock exchange was doing more business and a privatisation programme was slowly under way. It was not easy. Market reforms exposed previously protected firms to the cold wind of competition. These firms also had to service their debts at high rates of interest. About 1,000 firms were said to be at risk.

Tourism, which slumped during the Gulf war, was doing much better in 1993 and 1994. Two free ports at Bizerta and Zarzis were to be developed. The main exports were textiles, olive oil, phosphates, oil and chemicals, but there was a permanent trade deficit. Inflation in 1994 was about 6%. About 14% of the workforce was unemployed, posing by far the country's most serious problem. But GDP per head was, apart from some blips, growing steadily. It may not have been enjoying genuine multi-party democracy, but Tunisia in the mid-1990s was stable, basking in modest economic growth and slowly adapting to the free market.

Total area	163,610 sq km	% agricultural area	49
Capital	Tunis	Highest point metres	Kaf ash-
Other cities	Sfax, Bizerte		Sha'nabi 1,544
		Main rivers	Majardah

The economy

GDP $bn	15.3	GDP per head $	1,780
% av. ann. growth in		GDP per head in purchasing	
real GDP 1985–93	4.2	power parity $	5,070

Origins of GDP	% of total	Components of GDP	% of total
Agriculture	16.2	Private consumption	62.6
Industry	30.4	Public consumption	16.6
of which:		Investment	25.1
manufacturing	17.3	Exports	39.7
Services	53.4	Imports	-20.4

Production average annual change 1985–93, %

Agriculture	4.2	Manufacturing	6.4
Industry	3.8	Services	4.5

Inflation and exchange rates

Consumer price 1993 av. ann. incr.	4.5%	Dinars per $ av. 1994	1.01
Av. ann. rate 1988–93	6.4%	Dinars per SDR av. 1994	1.45

Balance of payments, reserves, aid and debt $bn

Visible exports fob	3.9	Capital balance	0.9
Visible imports fob	-6.0	Overall balance	0.001
Trade balance	-2.1	Change in reserves	0.002
Invisible inflows	2.7	Level of reserves end Dec.	0.9
Invisible outflows	-2.0	Foreign debt	8.7
Net transfers	0.7	as % of GDP	59.9
Current account balance	-0.8	Debt service	1.3
as % of GDP	-5.2	as % of export earnings	20.2

Principal exports 1993	$m fob	Principal imports	$m cif
Textiles & leather goods	1,763	Mechanical &	
Petroleum, gas & derivatives	432	electrical goods	1,878
Foodstuffs	397	Textiles & leather	1,318
Mechanical &		Petroleum, gas & derivatives	455
electrical goods	248	Iron & steel	420
Phosphates & fertilisers	223	Foodstuffs	416
Total	3,803	Total	5,839

Main export destinations	% of total	Main origins of imports	% of total
France	30.1	France	26.8
Germany	17.4	Italy	18.2
Italy	16.9	Germany	13.0
Belgium	7.3	United States	5.8
Libya	4.9	Belgium	4.4

Government

System Republic. Executive branch composed of president, prime minister and cabinet. President and unicameral Chamber of Deputies are elected simultaneously for a 5-year term.

Main political parties Rassemblement Constitutional Démocratique, Mouvement des Démocrates Socialistes, Rassemblement Socialiste Progressive, Parti de l'Unité Populaire, Parti Social pour le Progrès, Union Démocratique Unioniste, Mouvement de la Rénovation

Climate and topography

Temperate in north with mild, rainy winters and hot, dry summers. Desert in south. Mountains in north, dry central plain, south merges into Sahara.

People and society

Population m	8.4	% under 15	36.3
Pop. per sq km	51	% over 65	4.4
% urban	57	No. men per 100 women	102
% av. ann. growth 1987–92	1.9	Human Development Index	69
No. households m	...		

Life expectancy		Education	
Men	67 yrs	Spending as % of GDP	6.1
Women	69 yrs	Mean years of schooling	2.1
Crude birth rate	30	Adult literacy %	68.1
Crude death rate	7	Primary school enrolment %	117
Infant mortality rate	48	Secondary school enrolment %	46
Under-5 mortality rate	63	Tertiary education enrolment %	9

Workforce	% of total	Consumer goods ownership	
Services	40	Telephone mainlines per 1,000	38
Industry	34	Televisions per 100	8.1
Agriculture	26		
% of total population	30		

Ethnic groups	% of total	Religious groups	% of total
Arab-Berber	98	Muslim	98
European	1	Christian	1
Jewish	1		

Tourism		Health	
Tourist receipts $m	1,074	Pop. per doctor	1,870
		Low birthweight babies % of total	8
		Daily calories % of total requirement	137
		% pop. with access to safe water	70

UAE

Total area	83,600 sq km	Population	1.7m
GDP	$38.7bn	GDP per head	$22,470
Capital	Abu Dhabi	Other cities	Dubai, Sharjah, Ras al-Khaimah

They may be hot and humid, sparsely populated desert lands but it does not matter: the United Arab Emirates on the southern shores of the Gulf have three irresistible attractions: oil, gas and money. As the world oil price has gone down, the UAE's prosperity has been diminished. But not much.

History: a firm British hand

The UAE consists of seven sovereign states: Abu Dhabi, Ajman, Dubai, Fujairah, Ras al-Khaimah, Sharjah and Umm al-Qaiwan. It has a modest history. The Portuguese who had established trading posts in these parts were ousted in 1650 by the Dutch and subsequently the British. Nobody really ruled these lands, and the Gulf was infested with pirates, both European and Arab; its southern shores were called the pirate coast. But eventually the British took charge as they consolidated their control on India. They attacked the pirates' lair at Ras al-Khaimah, and they signed a treaty in 1820 with the Gulf sheikhs to end both piracy and slavery. A British naval squadron was assigned to Ras al-Khaimah. This did not end either piracy or slavery but the sheikhs saw the advantages of peace. So they agreed on a truce during the pearl-diving season (in 1835) and then a permanent truce (in 1853). Their lands became known as the Trucial States. Other European countries became interested in the area and began seeking influence. The British scotched this with a series of treaties in 1892 in which the sheikhs promised not to do any deals with foreign governments without British consent. The British retained the right to adjudicate frontiers. The man who mattered in the Trucial States was the British political agent in Dubai.

A fundamental change

In 1952 the British-officered Trucial Oman Scouts were set up as the basis for a regional security force. In the same year the sheikhs set up the Trucial Council to discuss their affairs in an organised way twice a year. The sheikhdoms were, at this time, under-developed and many of their inhabitants were illiterate nomads. Some of the sheikhs were very conservative: one of them, Shakhbut of Abu Dhabi, was said to keep all his money under his bed. All that changed with the discovery of oil in 1958 off the shore of Abu Dhabi and its production in commercial quantities in 1962. With discreet British help, Shakhbut (who had ruled since 1928) was deposed in 1966 and the modern-minded Sheikh Zayed took over. Oil was discovered in Dubai in 1966, in lesser quantities than in Abu Dhabi. The rulers of Abu Dhabi and Dubai took the lead among the sheikhdoms.

The next big change came in 1968 when Britain's Labour government announced it was withdrawing most of its forces from the Gulf by 1971. The sheikhs realised they were not powerful enough to deal with the outside world individually. Six of them formed a loose grouping which they called the United Arab Emirates in 1971 (and were joined by the seventh, Ras al-Khaimah, a year later). Britain's original idea had been to include two other Gulf sheikhdoms, Bahrain and Qatar. But they opted for separate independence. The state that emerged was led by Abu Dhabi. Its primacy was contested until his death by Dubai's Sheikh Rashid, who was also the UAE's prime minister. Under Rashid Dubai achieved great success as the region's leading entrepot. Sharjah experienced some dramas. In 1963 the conservative Sheikh Saqr was deposed by the less-conservative Sheik Khaled. The new ruler was killed in 1972 by followers of Saqr. After the rebels were captured, Khaled's brother took over and followed his relatively open-minded policies.

The move to centralisation

In the following years Abu Dhabi's Sheikh Zayed pressed forward with plans to centralise power. In 1973 a federal oil minister was appointed. Three years later three separate defence forces were linked up. Next came joint internal security and border controls, immigration and intelligence. But when in 1979 an Abu Dhabi-led majority called for abolishing internal borders and merging both the armed forces and the budgets, Dubai refused. After the eruption of the Iran-Iraq war, the Gulf's Arab rulers became concerned for their own security and formed the Gulf Co-operation Council (GCC) in 1981. In addition to the UAE its members are: Bahrain, Kuwait, Oman, Qatar and Saudi Arabia. One of the GCC's ideas was to strengthen the regional economy, perhaps creating a common market. But it paid most attention to military security. Member states began joint military exercises in 1983. They decided to form a "shield" against external aggression from Iraq or Iran. During the 1990 war to remove the Iraqi army from Kuwait, the GCC was firmly on the side of the American-led coalition forces.

Politics: no votes here

Under the constitution, the Supreme Council of the UAE is made up of the seven rulers. Its decisions must be taken with a majority of five votes, two of which must be those of Abu Dhabi and Dubai. Although it is the highest authority of the state it meets only once a year. It elects the president and his deputy. The composition of the Council of Ministers was agreed in 1971. It provides for six ministers from Abu Dhabi (including those for foreign affairs, the interior and information), three from both Dubai (defence, finance and industry) and Sharjah, two from Ajman and Umm al-Qaiwain and one from Fujairah. The late arrival, Ras al-Khaimah, was later given cabinet posts. There is a 40-member Federal National Council which could act as a sort of parliament since it reviews legislation sent to it by the Council of Ministers. But nobody in power has suggested that free democratic elections be held to this council. It is thought to be enough that citizens are granted automatic access to councillors from their part of the UAE. Political parties are banned.

Foreign policy: a watchful eye

The members of the UAE know they are held together by a fairly thin thread and are militarily weak yet surrounded by rich and powerful neighbours. The nearest of these, Saudi Arabia, is a friend and member of the GCC but its rulers have a tendency to bossiness. Iran, on the other side of the Gulf, looks scarily powerful and big. In 1972 the shah seized the islands of Abu Musa and the Greater and Lesser Tumbs, near the Strait of Hormuz, but subsequently Iran agreed to the shared use of Abu Musa and its oil. In 1992, however, Iran prevented a group of UAE teachers from landing on Abu Musa and asserted sovereignty over it. In response the UAE claimed sovereignty over all three islands, but could do little about it. On the other hand, Shia Muslim Iran has not tried to convert or take over the mainly Sunni Muslim UAE. Iraq, which started its war with Iran and invaded Kuwait, is seen by many in the UAE as a "mad dog" now mercifully chained up. With all of these concerns, defence spending in the UAE's 1992 budget reached 46% of the total.

Society: fear of foreigners

The indigenous people cling to loyalties to their rulers or members of the ruling family. They are sometimes united against the growing influence of foreigners who have better skills and do the more complicated jobs or who are prepared to do the dirty work which the locals disdain. In some areas, foreigners – Indians, Pakistanis, Yemenis, Palestinians, Sudanese and Iranians – are in a majority. By one unofficial reckoning they amount to over 80% of the total. There is no sign of Islamic extremism in the UAE: Islam is already an integral part of the way of life. Change may come to the UAE as increasing numbers of western-educated men and women come home and gain influential positions. As the number of schools expands the rate of illiteracy is being reduced: in 1992 the adult literacy rate was 65%.

Economy: oil and gas and over-spending

Abu Dhabi has nearly 10% of the world's crude oil reserves, or about 92,000m barrels at the end of 1992. In that year it produced 732m barrels of crude oil and 661,000m cubic feet of natural gas. Dubai's output (which will run out in 2009 unless more is found) and Sharjah's are much smaller. Not surprisingly there has been a tendency to over-spend. In 1987 plotters tried unsuccessfully to overthrow Sheikh Sultan of Sharjah on the ground that, even with Sharjah's oil revenues, he had incurred debts of $900m. Booming Dubai, on the other hand, has spent well on infrastructure. Dubai is what makes the UAE tick. Its non-oil trade has been growing at 20% a year. It caters for 70% of the UAE's total trade. Port Rashid has a turnaround time for container ships of 24 hours. Much of Dubai's big re-export trade by dhow and freighter from the famed Creek is to Iran, just across the Gulf. Dubai claims to be the "Hong Kong of the Gulf with echoes of Venice". But Abu Dhabi, with its skyscrapers and six-lane highways flanking the corniche with views across the Gulf, is not far behind.

The BCCI affair

In 1972 Sheikh Zayed helped a Pakistani banker, Agha Hassan Abedi, to found the Bank of Credit and Commerce International. In 1990 the government and ruling family increased their stake from 36% to 77%. In July 1991 the Bank of England and other banks, having found evidence of large-scale fraud, seized the BCCI's assets and closed it down. This left Abu Dhabi, where the bank had just been registered, to carry the can in dealings with the bank's enraged depositors. By mid-1995 the dispute had not been settled. It would eventually cost Abu Dhabi a huge sum of money. It may be hurting from lower world oil prices, like other producers, but Abu Dhabi can afford it.

Total area	83,600 sq km	% agricultural area	2
Capital	Abu Dhabi	Highest point metres	Jabal Hafit
Other cities	Dubai, Sharjah, Ras al-Khaimah		1,189

The economy

GDP $bn	38.7	GDP per head $	22,470
% av. ann. growth in real GDP 1985–92	1.7	GDP per head in purchasing power parity $	23,390

Origins of GDP	% of total	Components of GDP	% of total
Agriculture	2.0	Private consumption	...
Industry	56.0	Public consumption	...
of which:		Investment	127.5
manufacturing	9.0	Exports	62.4
Services	43.0	Imports	49.0

Production average annual change 1985–93, %

Agriculture	9.1	Manufacturing	3.3
Industry	-1.8	Services	4.1

Inflation and exchange rates

Consumer price 1993 av. ann. incr.	3.5%	Dirhams per $ av. 1994	3.67
Av. ann. rate 1988–93	3.6%	Dirhams per SDR av. 1994	5.27

Balance of payments, reserves, aid and debt

			$bn
Visible exports fob	23.0	Capital balance	...
Visible imports fob	-18.0	Overall balance	...
Trade balance	5.0	Change in reserves	...
Invisible inflows	...	Level of reserves end Dec.	6.0
Invisible outflows	...	Foreign debt	11.0
Net transfers	...	as % of GDP	30.9
Current account balance	2.0	Debt service	1.3
as % of GDP	5.2	as % of export earnings	6.5

Principal exports	$m fob	Principal imports	$m cif
Crude petroleum	13.6	Consumer goods	9.6
		Capital goods	6.1
		Intermediate goods	2.2
Total	23.0	Total	17.8

Main export destinations	% of total	Main origins of imports	% of total
Japan	35.9	Japan	13.4
United States	3.0	United Kingdom	9.5
France	0.9	United States	8.8
Germany	0.9	Germany	5.6

Government
System Federation of seven emirates represented by a Supreme Council of Rulers which elects the president and vice-president. The president appoints a Council of Ministers.
Main political parties none

Climate and topography
Desert climate. Flat, barren coastal plain merging into vast rolling sand dunes. Mountains in east are cooler.

People and society

Population m	1.7	% under 15	29.2
Pop. per sq km	20	% over 65	2.3
% urban	82	No. men per 100 women	187
% av. ann. growth 1987–92	3.4	Human Development Index	70.8
No. households m	...		

Life expectancy		Education	
Men	70 yrs	Spending as % of GDP	1.9
Women	74 yrs	Mean years of schooling	5.6
Crude birth rate	22	Adult literacy %	65
Crude death rate	4	Primary school enrolment %	115
Infant mortality rate	20	Secondary school enrolment %	69
Under-5 mortality rate	27	Tertiary education enrolment %	11

Workforce	% of total	Consumer goods ownership	
Services	57	Telephone mainlines per 1,000	...
Industry	38	Televisions per 100	11
Agriculture	5		
% of total population	50		

Ethnic groups	% of total	Religious groups	% of total
Emirian	19	Muslim	96
Other Arab	20	Christian & Hindu	4
South Asian	50		

Tourism		Health	
Tourist receipts $m	...	Pop. per doctor	1,040
		Low birthweight babies % of total	6
		Daily calories % of total requirement	151
		% pop. with access to safe water	100

YEMEN

Total area	527,970 sq km	Population	12.6m
GDP	$22.6bn	GDP per head	$1,089
Capital	Sanaa	Other cities	Aden, Hodeida, Mukalla

Yemen is a tragic, backward, divided and drug-addicted country where ideological and tribal disputes, sometimes provoked by ill-intentioned outsiders, are too often settled by the gun. After its latest civil war, in 1994, Yemen faces a heavy task of reconstruction.

History: there were some good times

In the first millenium BC Yemen was a centre of civilisation. It was famed for its conservation of water in terraces and dams (it had no great river flowing through the country). It was a trading post linking Asia, Africa and the Mediterranean. Control of the country was divided among various kingdoms and sultanates, the most famous of which was said to have been that of the legendary Queen of Sheba. According to Jewish and Islamic tradition she ruled southwest Arabia in the 10th century BC and at one time paid a visit to King Solomon, laden with jewels, to test his wisdom by asking him a series of riddles. Her name according to Islamic tradition was Bilqis.

Battleground in North Yemen

For much of its subsequent history Yemen was a battleground for warlords and religious leaders. Their dynasties came and went but Yemen did not prosper. One of the most well-established dynasties was that of the Zaydis, an austere Islamic family whose patriarch demanded absolute obedience from his followers. The Zaydis lived on the margins while others, including Egyptians and Turks, controlled populated areas. In the 17th century a Zaydi imam ousted the Turks but his power in Sanaa, the capital, faded; petty chieftains came to the fore in the south. The division between north and south largely came about because of rivalries between the Turkish and British empires in the 19th century.

Part of North Yemen was dominated until his assassination in 1948 by the puritanical and anti-British Imam Yahya, a Zaydi. The Zaydis held sway in North Yemen until 1962 when they were ousted in an army coup which led to the establishment of the Yemen Arab Republic. A civil war ensued between republicans supported by Egypt's President Nasser and royalists supported by Saudi Arabia. Nasser sent thousands of Egyptian troops to help. They left after Egypt's defeat by Israel in 1967 but the royalists had by that time faded into the hills. After two presidents were killed in 1978, Lieut-Colonel Ali Abdullah Saleh took charge and extracted aid from East and West.

Trouble in South Yemen too

In the 19th century Aden, then a village with potential as a harbour, fell under British influence owing to the far-sightedness of the British political agent there. It became a great coaling port for trade between Europe and Asia. In 1959 the British set up the Federation of South Arabia to give some coherence and stability to the collection of small, backward and weak sultanates of the area and two years later, worried about growing nationalism, they added Aden to it in the hope of strengthening it. But nationalism, stirred up by Nasser, who boasted that he would sweep the British out of South Arabia, was growing. The British decided to leave, and allowed the leftist National Liberation Front to take over in 1967. The new country became the People's Democratic Republic of Yemen and, eventually, the Arab world's lone Marxist state, subsidised by the Soviet Union. It was not monolithic, however. In 1986 a shoot-out in the ruling politburo led to a civil war in Aden in which thousands were killed or made homeless.

Unity, Yemeni-style

In 1990 Yemen became united under the "two Alis": President Ali Abdullah Saleh from the north and Vice-President Ali Salem al-Bayd from the south. The move was popular. People wanted an end to the troubles. Yemen had discovered oil and prospects looked better than anyone could remember (although Saudi Arabia was trying to scare off western oil companies by claiming that the oil was in disputed territory). Extraordinarily, free elections were held in an atmosphere of genuine political effervescence. Numerous political parties took part and there was a fairly free press. Mr Saleh's General People's Congress won 123 of the 301 seats in parliament; the conservative and puritanical Islah group won 62; and the (South) Yemen Socialist Party 56. The remainder went to independents. A three-way coalition was formed. This was political dynamite in a region where every other government was autocratic and brooked no opposition. It set a democratic example, implicitly challenging the legitimacy of the Gulf's ruling royal families, especially the one in neighbouring Saudi Arabia. To make matters worse, President Saleh appeared to side with Iraq when it invaded Kuwait and seemed poised to push into Saudi Arabia. The Saudis promptly cut off all aid to Yemen and cancelled the work permits of some 800,000 Yemeni immigrants, who had to return home.

Civil war, again

After weeks of sporadic skirmishes interspersed with unsuccessful attempts at mediation, another civil war erupted in 1994. Saudi Arabia was blamed in some western embassies for helping the southerners. But there had also been bitter disagreements between northern and southern leaders, and several of the southerners had been murdered. Significantly, the Saudis pressed Oman, which also has a border with Yemen, to recognise the southern separatist state (it did not). Disregarding calls for moderation, President Saleh vowed to crush the separatists, and did. It was all over in a couple of months. But in that time Aden was again badly damaged. The leader of the self-proclaimed "Democratic Republic of Yemen" fled to Oman and gave up politics. Where did this leave the new, northern-dominated Yemen? Almost certainly facing a resurgence of violence, sooner or later, from resentful defeated southerners. A sporadic border dispute with Saudi Arabia was settled in 1995.

Society: chewing their lives away

Yemeni society is poor and backward although there is a small but growing class of well-educated and articulate people who rejoiced in the democratic period before the 1994 civil war. The literacy rate for men is 53% and for women an appalling 26%. South Yemen's former communist government spent much more on education than President Saleh's in the north. The average number of children per mother is reckoned by the UN Development Programme to be 7.5, more than twice the world average.

Many thousands of people, more in the north than in the south and the eastern hills, chew *qat* every afternoon for several hours. *Qat* is a mild and cheap stimulant shrub. More men chew it than women. It causes euphoria followed by lethargy and is no help to productivity. The custom is widespread and something of an embarrassment to cultured Yemenis. The government publishes no statistics about its production and sale although it is taxed while on its way to market. *Qat* is one of the country's major crops if not the biggest. Demand for it is so strong that it provides employment for many farmers. Since Yemenis spend so much money on it, they have little left to save. The *Yemen*

Times reckoned in 1992 that the value added by the *qat* trade was roughly 25% of recorded GDP, annual *qat* output was about 250,000 tons and at least a quarter of irrigated land was dedicated to its cultivation. In a barren country where about 3% of the land is reckoned to be cultivable, this matters. Many farm products (less profitable to grow than *qat*) have to be imported.

The economy: oil and not much else

Not much is known about the economy, which is dominated by a small group of merchant families. Reliable statistics do not exist. Not only does *qat* go unrecorded, so does roughly half of the overall economy, which is untaxed and "black". There is a lot of smuggling to Saudi Arabia, especially of alcohol. Unification brought together two different economies: the southern communist one and the northern bumbling capitalist one. Nobody has a clear idea how that has been working out. Contracts for the refining of Iraqi and Kuwaiti oil at Aden were cancelled as a result of the Gulf war. The refinery was shelled by northern forces in 1994.

Unemployment is high. Apparently the Yemeni emigrants whom Saudi Arabia sent home were unskilled or semi-skilled; those who were skilled, and needed, were allowed to keep their jobs. The latest civil war was bound to lead to a reappraisal of their position by the two companies with the biggest investments: the American Hunt Oil and Canadian Occidental (CanOxy). They were likely to stay on, but others which had been thinking of investing might well have been deterred. CanOxy suspended liftings temporarily but also announced a new find. France's Total seemed undeterred and was talking of a pipeline from a field it had discovered. Output before the 1994 war was of about 375,000 barrels of crude a day.

A $5 billion project to exploit natural gas reserves, which might transform the economy, appeared to be a victim of the war. It had already been held up by a dispute between potential partners; investors were certain to "wait and see". The idea had been to run a pipeline to Aden, build a liquefaction plant there and ship the product to clients, perhaps in the Indian state of Maharashtra and in South Korea. Following the 1994 war, however, the victorious northerners were expected to insist on the pipeline going to the Red Sea coast, where they could be sure of controlling it.

Total area	527,970 sq km	% agricultural area	3.6
Capital	Sanaa	Highest point metres	Jabal an
Other cities	Aden, Hodeida,		Nabi Shu'ayb 3,760
	Mukalla	Main rivers	Wadi Hajr

The economy

GDP $bn	22.6	GDP per head $	1,089
% av. ann. growth in		GDP per head in purchasing	
real GDP 1985–93	...	power parity $	...

Origins of GDP	% of total	Components of GDP	% of total
Agriculture	21.0	Private consumption	68.4
Industry	24.0	Public consumption	28.5
of which:		Investment	20.0
manufacturing	10.6	Exports	14.9
Services	55.0	Imports	-31.9

Production average annual change 1985–93, %

Agriculture	...	Manufacturing	...
Industry	...	Services	...

Inflation and exchange rates

Consumer price 1993 av. ann. incr.	55.0%	Riyals per $ av. 1994	12.10
Av. ann. rate 1988–93	...	Riyals per SDR av. 1994	16.89

Balance of payments, reserves, aid and debt

			$bn
Visible exports fob	0.6	Capital balance	...
Visible imports fob	1.5	Overall balance	...
Trade balance	-0.9	Change in reserves	0.02
Invisible inflows	0.3	Level of reserves end Dec.	0.2
Invisible outflows	-0.9	Foreign debt	5.9
Net transfers	0.9	as % of GDP	56.4
Current account balance	-0.6	Debt service	0.5
as % of GDP	-2.8	as % of export earnings	7.5

Principal exports[a]	$m fob	Principal imports	$m cif
Mineral fuels & lubricants	457.00	Food & beverages	593.00
Food, beverages &		Manufactured goods	407.80
live animals	25.70	Machinery & transport	
Raw materials	19.20	equipment	345.00
		Fuels & lubricants	329.60
Total	1,200.00	Total	2,122.00

Main export destinations	% of total	Main origins of imports	% of total
Germany	27.9	United States	15.7
Japan	15.1	United Kingdom	6.7
United Kingdom	8.8	Japan	6.4
Austria	7.1	France	6.2
China	6.7	Italy	5.8

Government
System The president is head of executive branch, assisted by vice-president and council of ministers. Unicameral legislature directly elected for a 4-year term.
Main political parties General People's Congress, Yemeni Alliance for Reform, Yemen Socialist Party, Baath Party, Nasserite Unionists, Truth Party, United Democratic Front

Climate and topography
Hot and humid along west coast, temperate in mountains, hot, dry and harsh in east. Narrow coastal plain backed by flat-topped hills and rugged mountains. Desert plains in centre slope into desert interior of the Arabian peninsula.

People and society

Population m	12.6	% under 15	48.0
Pop. per sq km	24	% over 65	2.8
% urban	31	No. men per 100 women	99
% av. ann. growth 1987–92	3.3	Human Development Index	32.3
No. households m	1.4		

Life expectancy	yrs	Education	
Men	52	Spending as % of GDP	...
Women	53	Mean years of schooling	0.9
Crude birth rate	50	Adult literacy %	41
Crude death rate	15	Primary school enrolment %	76
Infant mortality rate	106	Secondary school enrolment %	31
Under-5 mortality rate	162	Tertiary education enrolment %	...

Workforce	% of total	Consumer goods ownership	
Services	26	Telephone mainlines per 1,000	11
Industry	11	Televisions per 100	2.9
Agriculture	63		
% of total population	25		

Ethnic groups	% of total	Religious groups	% of total
Arab	90	Shi'a Muslim	55
Afro-Arab	10	Sunni Muslim	45

Tourism		Health	
Tourist receipts $m	47	Pop. per doctor	...
		Low birthweight babies % of total	19
		Daily calories % of total requirement	93
		% pop. with access to safe water	36

a 1991.

Glossary

ADB African Development Bank. Multilateral development bank founded in 1963 and based in Abidjan, Côte d'Ivoire. Criticised for inefficiency partly caused by inadequate staffing.

Amal Moderate Shia Muslim militia in Lebanon led by Nabih Berri. Strongest in the south. Rival of Hizbullah.

Arab League Official name: The League of Arab States. Founded in Cairo in 1945 to co-ordinate the affairs of Arab governments. Ran boycott of trade with Israel. Arranges Arab summit meetings.

Arab Monetary Fund Founded in Abu Dhabi in 1977 as a first stage on the road to economic integration and to help needy member-governments, IMF-style.

Ayatollah Senior cleric in Iran's version of Shia Islam. Outranked only by an Imam or a Grand Ayatollah.

BADEA Arab Bank for Economic Development in Africa. Founded in Khartoum in 1973 by the Arab League.

Baath Arab socialist party. Has rival branches in Syria and Iraq.

Berber Indigenous people of North Africa now scattered through Morocco, Algeria, Libya and Egypt who survived Arab invasions. Have their own language and traditions.

Caliph Successor, or claimed successor, to the Prophet Muhammad.

Copt Member of the Coptic church, an Egypt-based Christian church with some 5m followers. Originated in 7th century. Copts have their own language, the Bohairic dialect of Alexandria. Have been occasionally persecuted by Islamists.

Council of Arab Economic Unity Founded in Amman in 1964 to pave the way for an Arab common market with standardised rules and regulations.

Dey Ruler of Tunis. Otherwise, a valiant military leader.

Druzes Small Middle Eastern Islamic sect based mainly in Lebanon. Has an eclectic and secret system of doctrines. Opposes inter-marriage. Has kept close-knit community for almost 1,000 years.

Empty Quarter Vast unpopulated desert in Saudi Arabia.

Ennadha Banned Islamist party in Tunisia.

FAO Food and Agriculture Organisation of the United Nations. Founded in 1945 and based in Rome. Provides technical assistance on agricultural production.

Fatah Mainstream faction of the Palestine Liberation Organisation, led by Yasser Arafat.

FIS Islamic Salvation Front. Won local elections in Algeria in 1990 and was about to win general elections in 1991 when the armed forces took over, provoking an upsurge in violence.

FLN National Liberation Front. Originally a rebel army opposed to French rule in Algeria. Took power after independence and imposed one-party socialism.

Gamaat Islamiya Islamic Group. One of two main violent Islamic extremist organisations in Egypt.

Great Man-Made River Vast project by Libya's leader, Colonel Muammar Qaddafi, to pump water from aquifers under the Sahara desert and deliver it to Tripoli, Benghazi and other coastal towns.

Gulf (The) Neutral word frequently used to refer to what is also known as the Persian Gulf and the Arabian Gulf.

Gulf Co-operation Council Official name: Co-operation Council for the Arab States of the Gulf. Six-nation group founded in Riyadh in 1981 to establish close co-operation on trade and security matters. Members are: Saudi Arabia, Kuwait, Qatar, Bahrain, the United Arab Emirates and Oman.

Gulf war Fought between 1980 and 1988 with huge losses on both sides by Iraq, which launched it, and Iran, which had appeared to provoke Iraq. Nobody won. Another Gulf war took place in 1991 following Iraq's invasion of Kuwait.

Haj Arabic for pilgrimage to Mecca.

Haran mosque In the centre of Mecca. Contains the black stone (Ka'aba) revered by Muslims.

Hashemite Member of the House of Hashem. Its leader, Sherif Hussein, amir of Mecca (1916–24), claimed to be a successor of the Prophet and proclaimed himself to be king of the Hejaz (comprising Jeddah, Mecca and Medina). King Hussein of Jordan, who says that his is a Hashemite kingdom, is Sherif Hussein's great grandson.

Hejaz The area ruled by Sherif Hussein (see above) until he was ousted by Ibn Saud, who absorbed the region into his new kingdom of Saudi Arabia.

Hizbullah Shia Muslim extremist group based in Lebanon. Main goal is to force Israel to withdraw its forces from the security zone imposed by Israel north of its border with Lebanon.

Hojatoleslam Iranian clerical rank held by President Rafsanjani which is lower than that of ayatollah.

ICO Islamic Conference Organisation. Founded in Saudi Arabia, in 1971, defends and promotes the presence of Islam in the world through holding summit meetings and co-operation.

Intifada Popular uprising against Israeli occupation and rule in the Gaza strip and West Bank. Consisted mainly of stone-throwing by youths and closures of shops.

Islamic Development Bank Based in Jeddah and founded in 1973 the bank gives loans primarily but not exclusively for development projects in Islamic countries while adhering to the Islamic principle forbidding usury.

Jihad Arabic for holy war.

Ka'aba Sacred black stone in Mecca's Haran mosque, revered by Muslims on pilgrimage who seek to kiss it.

Khalifa Ruling family in Bahrain.

Kurds Ethnic group, mainly Sunni Muslim, scattered through contiguous parts of Turkey, Iran and Iraq. About 9m–10m. Have lived in "Kurdistan" for millennia. Hardy fighters. Seek at least autonomy for their regions.

Levant Word used to describe the region along the southeast Mediterranean coast including Syria, Lebanon and Israel.

Likud Conservative Israeli political grouping traditionally taking a harder line on relations with the Palestinians than the Labour Party. Has provided Israel with two prime ministers, Menachem Begin and Yitzhak Shamir.

Maghreb Africa north of the Sahara desert, comprising Morocco, Algeria, Tunisia and Libya.

Maronites Members of Christian church whose name originates either with St Maron, a Syrian hermit of the 5th century, or with Ioannes Maron, patriarch of Antioch in 685–707. The Maronites, whose language is Arabic, use the ancient West Syrian liturgy in their services. Some Maronites, having fled persecution, are scattered around the world. But the bulk have remained and play a central role in Lebanese political life.

Mecca Most holy city of Islam. Home of the Haran mosque where the sacred black stone, the Ka'aba, is kept. The Prophet Muhammad said he had received revelations from the Angel Jibril while meditating in the Cave of Hira, near the summit of the Mountain of Light, close to Mecca.

Medina Holy city of Islam where the Prophet Muhammad lived, preached and is buried.

Mesopotamia Area in Iraq between the Tigris and Euphrates rivers.

Muslim Brotherhood Long-established Egyptian Islamist grouping.

OAPEC Organisation of Arab Petroleum Exporting Countries. Founded in Kuwait in 1968 to protect the interests of Arab oil-producing countries.

OPEC Organisation of Petroleum Exporting Countries. Founded in Vienna in 1960 to co-ordinate production quotas with a view to keeping the world price as high as possible.

Passover Jewish feast day commemorating the "passing

over" of the houses of the Israelites when the Egyptians, their captors, who had refused God's order to free them, were smitten with the loss of their firstborn.

Phoenicians Ancient people of the eastern Mediterranean based in Tyre and Sidon, in what is now Lebanon. Acquired a reputation as astute traders. Travelled and settled in parts of the eastern Mediterranean and Middle East.

PLO Palestine Liberation Organisation. Chairman: Yasser Arafat. Umbrella group including Arafat's mainstream Fatah faction and several hard-line groups opposed to Arafat and based in Syria.

PNC Palestine National Council. Loose, appointed but broadly representative assembly, rarely convened, of Palestinians living in the Gaza strip and West Bank and those in the *diaspora*.

Polisario Rebel group opposed to Morocco's takeover of the formerly Spanish Western Saharra.

Qaboos (Sultan) Ruler of Oman.

Qat A mild and cheap stimulant shrub chewed daily by a large portion of the population in Yemen.

Ramadan The ninth month of the Muslim year, rigidly observed as a 30 days' fast, during the hours of daylight, by all Muslims.

Rushdie (Salman) Author of *The Satanic Verses*. Sentenced to death, *in absentia*, for profanity by Ayatollah Khomeini.

Sabah Name of the Kuwaiti ruling family.

Sabra (1) One of two Palestinian refugee camps (the other was Chatila) in Beirut where in 1982 Maronite Christian militiamen slaughtered hundreds of unarmed civilian men, women and children before the eyes of Israeli soldiers following the forced departure from Beirut of Lebanon-based Palestinian fighters. (2) Name given to Israelis who were born before 1948 in Palestine or after 1948 in Israel.

Shatt al-Arab Major waterway, which has been contested by Iran and Iraq, carrying part of the waters of the Euphrates and Tigris rivers to the Gulf and giving marine access to Abadan (Iran) and Basra (Iraq).

Shia Second strand of Islam after the Sunni Muslims (see below). The Shia comprise roughly 60m–80m believers. They are in the majority in Iran, Iraq and possibly Yemen. They differ from Sunni Muslims in that they say the line of succession after the Prophet Muhammad went to his son-in-law, Ali, and not to the first four caliphs of Islam (Ali was the fifth). Some of the Shia are "Twelvers". They believe that Muhammad al-Mahdi, the 12th imam (true successor to the Prophet, of whom Ali was the first), did not die and is in fact the "hidden imam". They believe he will reappear before Judgment Day and rule, as a sort of Messiah, by divine right. Shia Islam is virtually universal in Iran. Elsewhere in the Islamic world its followers have taken second place in terms of power and influence to Sunni Muslims, in Iraq and Lebanon for example. The Shia have, however, been making major advances in Lebanon.

Six-day war Took place in 1967 after Egypt ordered the departure of a peace force on the border with Israel and closed the Gulf of Aqaba, Israel's outlet to the Red Sea. Responding to what it saw as an act of war, Israel destroyed the air forces of its Arab adversaries and seized the Sinai desert, the West Bank, the Gaza strip and the Golan Heights.

SLA South Lebanon Army. Set up, trained and financed by Israel to defend Israel's "security zone" in south Lebanon until the Lebanese government could guarantee that the area would not be used by guerrillas to launch attacks across the border.

SOLIDERE Lebanese redevelopment company, whose principal investor is said to be the prime minister, Rafik Hariri. Has launched huge project to redevelop the ruined city centre of Beirut.

Sultan Hereditary ruler, as in Oman (Sultan Qaboos).

Sunni One of the two major branches of Islam. The other is Shia (see above). Sunni Muslims comprise about nine tenths of all Muslims. They recognise the first four caliphs of Islam as the rightful successors to the Prophet Muhammad. Shia Muslims think the successor to the Prophet was his son-in-law, Ali. Sunni Muslims view the state envisaged by Muhammad to be earthly and pragmatic rather than divinely inspired. Thus Sunni Muslims accepted rulers in Mecca of varying quality provided that they could keep order and serve as guardians for the correct practise of Islam. Sunni Islam emphasizes the views of the majority but does not hesitate to adapt and add views and customs as the faith evolves. There are more than 300m Sunni Muslims.

Thani Sheikh Khalifa bin Hamad al-Thani is Ruler of Qatar.

UNDOF UN Disengagement Observer Force. Monitors the disangagement of Israeli and Syrian forces at the Golan Heights.

UNESWA UN Economic and Social Commission for Western Asia. Established in Baghdad in 1974 to collate and produce information about the Middle East.

UNIFIL UN Interim Force in Lebanon. Established in 1978. Large (about 5,000–6,000) force based in south Lebanon

---

and intended to provide stability and monitor the departure of Israeli forces and their replacement by Lebanese army.

UNRWA   UN Relief and Works Administration. Founded in Vienna in 1950. Provides help to Palestinian refugees in the Gaza strip, West Bank, Jordan, Lebanon and Syria.

UNTSO   UN Truce Supervision Organisation. Set up in Jerusalem to monitor a 1948 ceasefire. Now performs several monitoring duties for the UN in the region.

Wafd   Long-standing Egyptian opposition party.

Wahabi   Name of sect espousing the sternly puritanical vision of Islam taught by Muhammad bin Abdul Wahab in the 18th century in what is now Saudi Arabia.

Yom Kippur   Day of atonement. One of Jewry's High Holy Days. Egypt launched its Yom Kippur war, when the Israelis were least prepared for it, in 1973.

Notes on data

For a list of the main sources used in preparing this book see page 166.

Coverage

The extent and quality of the statistics available vary from country to country. Every care has been taken to specify the broad definitions on which the data are based and to indicate cases where data quality or technical difficulties are such that interpretation of the figures is likely to be seriously affected. Nevertheless, figures from individual countries will often differ from standard international statistical definitions.

Statistical basis

The research for this section was carried out in 1995 using the latest published sources. The data, therefore, unless otherwise indicated, refer to the year ending December 31st 1993. Exceptions are: population under 15 and over 65, number of men per 100 women and urban population which refer to estimates for 1992; crude birth and death rates and life expectancy are based on 1985–90 averages; workforce and tourism refer to 1992; ethnic groups, religious groups, consumer goods ownership, education and health data refer to the latest year with available figures.

Figures may not add exactly to totals, or percentages to 100, because of rounding. Sums of money have generally been converted to US dollars at the official exchange rate ruling at the time to which the figures refer.

Some countries do not appear in rankings because no data was available for a comparable period.

Definitions

Agricultural area The area of arable land, land under permanent crops and pasture land expressed as a percentage of a country's total area.

Balance of payments The record of a country's transactions with the rest of the world. The **current account** of the balance of payments consists of: exports of visible trade (goods) less imports of visible trade; "invisible" trade: receipts and payments for services such as banking, tourism and shipping plus dividend and interest payments and profit remittances; private transfer payments, such as remittances from those working abroad; official transfers, including payments to international organisations and some current expenditure aid flows (such as famine relief). Visible imports and exports are normally compiled on rather different definitions to those used in the trade statistics (shown in principal imports and exports) and therefore the statistics do not match. The **capital account** consists of long- and short-term transactions relating to a country's assets and liabilities (for example loans and borrowings). Adding the current to the capital account gives the overall balance. This is compensated by net monetary movements and changes in reserves. In practice methods of statistical recording are neither complete nor accurate and an errors and omissions item, sometimes quite large, will appear. In the country facts pages of this book this item is included in the overall balance. Changes in reserves are shown without the practice of reversing the sign often followed in balance of payments presentations. They exclude monetary movements and therefore do not equal the overall balance.

Cif/fob When goods pass through customs and are recorded in trade statistics they are normally registered at their value at the point of passage through customs. Imports, which are valued at the point of entry to a country, will include the cost of "carriage, insurance and freight" (cif) from the exporting country to the importing one. The value of exports does not include these elements and is recorded "free on board" (fob). The value of imports will therefore automatically be greater than the equivalent amount of exports – in many cases by a factor of 10–12%. In most (but not all) countries the crude trade statistics record imports cif and exports fob; balance of payments statistics are generally adjusted so that imports are shown fob.

Crude birth rate The number of live births in a year per 1,000 population. The crude rate will automatically be relatively high if a large proportion of the population is of childbearing age and low if this is not the case.

Crude death rate The number of deaths in one year per 1,000 population. Like the crude birth rate this is affected by the population's age structure. It will be relatively high if there is a high proportion of old people in the population.

Debt, foreign Financial obligations owed by a country to the rest of the world and repayable in foreign currency.

Debt service consists of interest payments on outstanding debt plus any principal repayments due. What is paid, of course, is not always what is due. **The debt service ratio** is debt service expressed as a percentage of the country's earnings from exports of goods and services.

Enrolment ratio (gross) The number enrolled at a specific level of education, whether or not they belong to the age group relevant to that level, as a percentage of the total population in the relevant age group. The ratio can therefore be over 100% if children start an education stage early or stay in it late; conversely, a ratio below 100% can be consistent with full education if children of the appropriate age group have passed on early to the following stage.

GDP Gross Domestic Product. It is the sum of all output produced by economic activity within that country. Economic activity normally refers to goods and services that are exchanged for money or traded in a market system (activities such as housework, childcare by parents and household repairs or improvements carried out by occupiers are excluded). Subsistence farming and other activities that could potentially be exchanged for money are theoretically also included but national statistics vary in the extent to which they cover them.

GDP can be measured in three ways: by summing the output of all production (origins of GDP); by measuring all expenditure on a country's production and adding stockbuilding (components of GDP); or by measuring the income of businesses and individuals generated by the production of goods and services. The exports and imports figures shown in national accounts statistics are defined differently from visible and invisible exports and imports used in the balance of payments, notably by excluding interest, profits and dividends payments.

GDP can be measured either at "market prices", the prices at which goods and services are bought by consumers, or at "factor cost", the cost of producing an item excluding taxes and subsidies. In general the expenditure breakdown is shown at market prices and the production breakdown at factor cost. Data on total GDP generally refer to market prices.

National income is obtained by deducting an estimate of depreciation of capital goods (capital consumption) from GDP.

The average annual increase in real GDP shows the growth in GDP excluding any increase due solely to the rise in prices.

Human Development Index This index is an attempt by the United Nations Development Programme to assess relative levels of human development in various countries. It combines three measures: life expectancy, literacy and whether the average income, based on purchasing power parity (PPP) estimates (see below), is sufficient to meet basic needs. For each component a country's score is scaled according to where it falls between the minimum and maximum country scores; for income adequacy the maximum is taken as the official "poverty line" incomes in nine industrial countries. The scaled scores on the three measures are averaged to give the Human Development Index, shown here scaled from 0 to 100. Countries scoring less than 50 are classified as low human development, those from 50 to 80 as medium and those above 80 as high.

As with any statistical exercise of this sort the results are subject to caveats and the small number of indicators used places some limitations on its usefulness. The index should not be taken as a quality of life indicator since in particular it excludes any direct notion of freedom.

Infant mortality The number of deaths of infants under 1-year old per 1,000 live births.

Inflation The rate at which prices are increasing. The most common measure and the one shown here (but not the only one) is to take the increase in the consumer price index.

Life expectancy rates refer to the average length of time a baby born today can expect to live.

PPP Purchasing Power Parity. Comparing GDP per head is an unsatisfactory way of comparing relative living standards since it does not take account of differences in prices of goods and services (the cost of living). PPP statistics adjust for cost of living differences by replacing normal exchange rates with rates designed to equalize the prices of a standard "basket" of goods and services. These are used to obtain PPP estimates of GDP per head, which are expressed in dollar terms or on a scale of 1–100, taking the United States as 100.

Real terms Figures adjusted to allow for inflation.

Under-5 mortality rate The number of deaths of children under 5 years of age per 1,000 live births averaged over the previous 5 years.

Abbreviations

bn	billion (one thousand million)	m	million
GDP	Gross Domestic Product	PPP	Purchasing Power Parity
GNP	Gross National Product	–	zero
kg	kilogram	...	not available
km	kilometre		

Sources

EIU, *Country Reports and Country Risk Service*

Encyclopedia Britannica

The Europa World Yearbook

IMF, *Balance of Payments Yearbook*

IMF, *International Financial Statistics*

International Labor Office, *Yearbook of Labor Statistics*

Statesmens's Year-Book

United Nations, *World Population Prospects*

United Nations Development Programme, *Human Development Report*

US Central Intelligence Agency, *World Factbook*

World Bank, *Trends in Developing Economies*

World Bank, *World Debt Tables*

World Bank, *World Development Report*

World Bank, *World Population Prospects*

World Bank, *World Tables*

Inset